World Bank Occasional Papers

NUMBER THREE, NEW SERIES

World Bank Occasional Papers, New Series

Subsidizing Industrial Location

A Conceptual Framework with Application to Korea

Michael P. Murray

Published for The World Bank

THE JOHNS HOPKINS UNIVERSITY PRESS

Baltimore and London

©1988 The International Bank
for Reconstruction and Development / THE WORLD BANK
1818 H Street, N.W., Washington, D.C. 20433, U.S.A.
All rights reserved
Manufactured in the United States of America
First printing November 1988

The Johns Hopkins University Press
Baltimore, Maryland 21211, U.S.A.

The findings, interpretations, and conclusions expressed in this study are the
results of research supported by the World Bank, but they are entirely those of
the author and should not be attributed in any manner to the World Bank, to
its affiliated organizations, or to members of its Board of Executive Directors
or the countries they represent.

Library of Congress Cataloging-in-Publication Data

Murray, Michael P., 1946–
   Subsidizing industrial location.

   (World Bank occasional papers ; new ser., no. 3)
   Bibliography: p.
   1. Korea (South)—Industries—Location—Government
policy—Econometric models.   I. Title.   II. Series.
HC470.D5M87   1988   338.6′042′095195   88-45375
ISBN 0-8018-3752-9

Contents

Preface

MANY GOVERNMENTS attempt to alter the spatial pattern of economic activity in their countries by giving subsidies or imposing taxes to induce firms to select preferred locations. The World Bank, in collaboration with the Seoul National University Graduate School of Environmental Studies, undertook a comprehensive study of industrial location policies in the Republic of Korea in order to offer good counsel to Korean policymakers and to glean from the Korean experience lessons applicable in other developing countries.

The study was directed by Kyu Sik Lee, and I was one of the researchers he selected. He asked me to review the literature on urban and public economics for what it had to say about the evaluation of industrial location policies. My search through the literature was dismaying. J. V. Henderson had indeed developed a general model for analyzing the optimal configuration of cities by size, but he concluded that formal economic models offer little quantitative insight into the best spatial arrangement of economic activity.

Unable to assess how well policies achieve governments' goals, I shifted my attention to how well governments choose instruments for their policies. Most governments use numerous carrots and sticks to influence firms' choices of location: government subsidies and taxes sometimes affect land, sometimes labor, and sometimes capital. I found that an adaptation of the classical analysis of optimal taxation offered an empirically tractable way to compare alternative subsidy mechanisms. This book makes that comparison.

I am grateful to Kyu Sik Lee for his support, encouragement, and counsel throughout this project. Heon Park and David Glyer of Claremont Graduate School provided me with able research assistance. I owe a special intellectual debt to Stephen Kennedy, who explained to me his theoretical work on consumer subsidies a decade ago; in preparing this monograph I unconsciously rediscovered some of his insights in the context of the firm. At various stages of my research, J. V. Henderson, William

Naught, Edwin Mills, George Tolley, and four anonymous reviewers all offered helpful suggestions. Sang-Choel Choe of Seoul National University, the local project director, and his graduate students provided data essential to the simulations I report. Diane Reedy did a comprehensive review of the literature to obtain parameter values from other studies. Lori Harnack provided expert clerical support, and Rosanne Ducey gave me valuable editorial assistance. Many of the strengths of the monograph are due to these people; all of the weaknesses are due to me. With love and admiration, I dedicate the book to Marie FitzGerald Murray and Thomas J. Murray.

Introduction

POLICYMAKERS IN the Republic of Korea give much attention to industrial location. The rationales for this concern are numerous: the proximity of the capital city, Seoul, to the border of the Democratic People's Republic of Korea makes industry around the capital particularly vulnerable; congestion and pollution in Seoul lead some to believe the city is too densely configured; and regional disparities in living standards raise questions about the appropriateness of the Seoul region's economic dominance. But even more striking than the number of reasons offered for government intervention are the variety and number of devices the government uses to influence the choice of industrial location. Mandates, prohibitions, tax breaks, loan guarantees, grants, land price reductions, promises of public infrastructure investments, and wage bill subsidies are all found in the grab bag of carrots and sticks used to alter the spatial outcomes of the marketplace.

In a random survey of 141 establishments that had moved within the Seoul region, eleven government programs were cited by respondents as having affected the firms' location decisions.[1] One cannot help but ask both whether some of these programs are better than others, and under what circumstances one is preferable to another.

Most radically, one might ask whether the Korean government should try to influence firms' location decisions at all. Policies that focus on these decisions may be heavy-handed substitutes for alternative policies that more directly address the concerns of the government. For example, a dense concentration of firms often causes objectionable levels of pollution. But taxes on the pollutants generated, rather than instruments to deconcentrate the firms, are generally the socially least costly mechanism for reducing such pollution. Direct intervention in firms' location choices is the "best" strategy for the government in only limited circumstances.

Unfortunately, there is no carefully articulated conceptual framework for analyzing the full effects of industrial location policies. Moreover, the theoretical literatures on industrial spatial choice and on optimal city size suggest that an appropriate framework would be cumbersome and would yield little in the way of analytical insights. Henderson (1980) finds that models of optimal city size are very sensitive to small changes in households' tastes and firms' technologies; given the state of the art of estimating tastes and technologies, estimates of what cities should look like will be unreliable.

In any event, policymakers should be cautioned that location policies may not do much to alter the spatial configurations of cities in market-oriented economies. Despite the large number of relatively generous schemes offered by the Korean government, most intraregional moves by Seoul firms are conducted without aid from government programs. Indeed, in the 1981 Korean national survey of manufacturing firms, 74 percent of the firms that had moved reported that they had done so primarily for operational reasons; only 12 percent reported that they had moved primarily in response to government subsidies or relocation mandates. If extensive location policies such as those in Korea have only marginal effects on the location decisions of firms, no governments can expect to alter greatly the spatial configurations of their manufacturing sectors without virtually abandoning free market mechanisms.

Potentially more fruitful than asking *whether* to move a firm from A to B is to ask *how* to move it. This is in fact the question a policymaker is more likely to pose to economists. Should the government subsidize the interest rates paid by a firm if it moves—or subsidize land prices instead? Is a subsidy on wages to be preferred to a public investment in sewers or roads? In Korea and throughout the developing world industrial location is a politically charged issue, and politicians are unlikely to turn to technicians for any advice except how to achieve their goal.

But the question of how can still be economically important. Simulations reported below show that, to induce a given relocation decision, subsidizing interest rates can be twice as costly as subsidizing the price of land! But this gets us ahead of ourselves. Before we can evaluate or appreciate the results of such simulations, we need to work our way through the theoretical and empirical exercises that underlie them. This is the task of the coming chapters.

Note

1. The World Bank–Seoul National University Project Survey of 500 manufacturing establishments, conducted in 1981.

CHAPTER 1

A Framework for Analysis

A SUCCESSFUL INDUSTRIAL location policy induces a firm that would have chosen location A to choose location B, which the government prefers. The policy must overcome any cost or profit advantage that site A enjoys. The essential economic question is, "How costly is it for the government to achieve a switch in the relative profitability of site B and site A?" In choosing among alternative policies, the question becomes, "Which politically feasible policy most cheaply overcomes site A's advantage?"

Many economists' likely first response to these questions is to argue that a simple cash payment to the firm, one just large enough to offset site A's advantage, is the most efficient (that is, least costly) policy. There is a certain naïveté in this response, however. The political process often restricts the policies available to government: cash payments by the government to private firms for cooperating with government policies are frequently politically unacceptable. Even when direct payments are not completely out of the question, their political costs may outweigh their economic advantages.

The argument in favor of cash grants is that they leave the firm, once it has moved to site B, with its incentives intact to produce its output as cheaply as possible. Many other policies do not share this virtue.

Location Distortion

All policies that induce the firm to locate at B distort the location outcomes of the free market. Such distortions are not costless. The firm had reasons for initially preferring site A: either revenues would be less at site B (consumers would place less value on the firm's product at B), or costs would be higher (more of society's resources would be absorbed in producing the firm's output at B). In either case, the decline in profits in going from A to B reflects a real social cost of locating at B rather than

5

A. This social cost is a "location distortion" caused by a policy that entices the firm to locate at B rather than A.

Countering this social cost of using site B are the social benefits of having the firm at B rather than at A—the benefits (such as reduced congestion or greater national security) that motivated the government policy in the first place. A fundamental criterion for good policies is that these social benefits outweigh the social costs.

The costs of relocation may be either borne by the government or imposed on the firm. For example, if site A is $100 more profitable than site B, a government subsidy of, say, a lump sum of $150 to the firm will induce the firm to relocate, but the firm might also locate at B if the government prohibited it from choosing site A. In both cases, the move has a social cost of $100, but that cost is borne by government in the former case and by the firm in the latter case.

In this subsidy case, treasury costs exceed the social costs by $50, and the subsidy has two components: a relocation grant of $100 compensating the firm for its lost profits and a pure transfer of $50 from the treasury to the firm. Knowing the difference in potential profitability of the two sites enables one to assess what part of a given relocation subsidy is needed to bring about the change in location and what part is a pure transfer to the recipient.

Differences in profitability between locations can arise from differences in output or input prices, in location-specific tax liabilities, and in the quantities of fixed inputs (public or private) available at each site. Such differences may arise from differences in transportation costs to and from markets, from the comparative advantages of the locations themselves, or from public or private infrastructure already in place.

Because the differences between sites have specific roots, governments frequently tailor specific policies to overcome them. This in part accounts for the plethora of relocation policies used by many governments. Some industrial location policies offer transportation subsidies to reduce the disadvantage of remote locations. Some subsidize wage payments to labor to offset higher skilled labor costs in less developed regions. Others subsidize capital costs to compensate for a lack of infrastructure. Still others offer to increase the public provision of goods or services to close the gap between rich and poor regions.

Production Distortion

The compensatory policies just mentioned (and others like them) differ from those that prohibit a move or offer a cash subsidy. Compensatory policies not only induce the firm to choose site B rather than A, but they also alter either relative factor prices or relative input availabilities at B. Consequently, these policies may also distort the *production* decisions of the firm after it does locate at B.

A firm prohibited from locating at A will choose the cheapest possible way to produce its output at B. If market prices reflect marginal social costs, this implies that the firm will minimize the social cost of producing its output.[1] If the government location policy alters factor prices from their market levels, however, the bundle of inputs chosen by the firm to minimize its own outlays will no longer minimize the social cost of production. The difference between the lowest cost at which production at B could be achieved and the cost of the resources actually chosen by the firm (given government policies) is what we refer to as the "production distortion" caused by the policies. Any production distortion will increase the total social cost of the location policy beyond the cost of the location distortion already discussed.

As an illustration, consider a firm whose output and revenue would be the same at B as at A, so that differences in profits at A and B arise only from differences in costs. If the firm were to operate at B and face market prices, $P_{B_i}^m$, for inputs, it would choose inputs X^o. If input prices paid by the firm were altered by the location policy, however, it would choose a different bundle of inputs, X^s. For example, a wage subsidy to the firm would induce the firm to use more labor and less of some other inputs. The true value of the resources used by the firm under the subsidy scheme would be

$$\sum_{i=1}^{n} P_{B_i}^m X_i^s$$

that is, their cost reckoned at market prices. But the output *could* have been produced for as little as

$$\sum_{i=1}^{n} P_{B_i}^m X_i^o$$

that is, the costs the firm would have incurred for different inputs if it had faced market prices. Consequently, the social cost of the production distortion would be the difference between these two sums.

Comparing Policies

In general, the social benefits that the government envisions from an altered spatial pattern of industrial activity must be balanced against both components of the cost of relocation, location distortion and production distortion. When two policy devices that would achieve the same reordering of industrial location are compared, however, production distortion becomes the only relevant consideration because location distortions are identical. The discussion which follows focuses on the production distortions caused by relocation policies because production distortions will determine the answer to a policymaker's query, "Should I undertake policy X or policy Y to get firms to locate at B rather than A?"

Location distortions do not, however, drop out of the picture altogether. Each potentially successful subsidy policy must provide a firm with enough benefits to overcome site B's cost disadvantage; it is the location distortion that will determine this threshold level for each policy option. A policymaker cannot simply ask, "Which is cheaper, to subsidize capital purchases ten cents on the dollar or land purchases fifteen cents on the dollar?" If ten cents on the dollar for capital purchases will not make the firm move, it is irrelevant whether this policy would be cheaper. And if fifteen cents on the dollar for land purchases is more costly because two cents on the dollar would suffice to induce the firm to move, then it is still not known which is better, subsidizing capital or subsidizing land. The relevant question is, "Which is cheaper, a price subsidy on capital that just overcomes the cost advantage of A or a price subsidy on land that just overcomes the cost advantage of A?"

Price subsidies are not the only tools used by governments. The relevant question may also take the form, "Which is cheaper, a price subsidy on capital that just overcomes the cost advantage of A or social infrastructure investments at B that just overcome the cost advantage of A?"

"Subsidizing factor prices" or "spending government money on plant or infrastructure" are succinct phrases that actually apply to many industrial location policies in Korea and elsewhere. The following examples illustrate how one might analyze specific policies.

An *investment tax credit* for new plant and equipment at the new location reduces the price of capital goods. In effect, it will increase the use of these inputs relative to labor and other inputs. It will confer greater benefits on firms that use more capital or that find it easier to substitute capital for other inputs.

Analyzing the social cost of an investment tax credit thus entails two steps. First, the differences in profitability between the old and new site must be computed to ascertain the location distortion induced by the policy. Second, the production distortion resulting from an inappropriate input mix must also be calculated; this requires comparing the true value of inputs chosen by the firm with the value of the inputs which would be chosen if the firm were not confronted with an artificially low price of capital.

Relocation assistance funds may be provided in proportion to the value of the plant at the previous location. Because such grants are independent of factor usage at the new location, they induce no production distortion. These grants obviously confer greater benefits on firms who use more capital than others, but to the extent that the firm's plant is immobile, these greater benefits accompany greater opportunity cost in abandoning the old site. Analyzing the social cost of this measure requires only a calculation of the location distortion.

A *capital gains tax exemption* on the properties (plant and land) disposed of at the previous location induces no production distortion because the exemption is independent of factor choices at the new location; the social cost of the policy is equal to the location distortion. But capital gains are likely to be only loosely tied to the immobility of the firm. Consequently, unlike relocation assistance funds, exemptions from taxes on capital gains are unlikely to offer greater benefits to firms for which moving is more costly. Indeed, firms with immobile, specialized capital are likely to suffer capital losses in abandoning their former site (unless, of course, they simply sell to someone else who will engage in the same specialized activity, thereby largely thwarting the intent of the policy). Consequently, this measure is likely to confer the largest benefits on those who need it least and the smallest benefits on those who need it most.

An *income tax exemption* for an individual whose entire family relocates with the firm effectively lowers the wage rate paid by the firm because it at least partially compensates the employee for relocating with the firm. The measure suggests several possible scenarios.

First, it is possible that some workers will refuse to relocate and will change jobs. They may judge that the prevailing wage in the new location, even when untaxed, is too low to compensate them for switching locations.

Second, it is possible that some workers will relocate with their employer and accept a wage at or below the prevailing wage in the new location. These workers may judge that the tax break makes the new location better than the old. If the workers must keep the same employer to receive the tax break, then the employer need pay them only the minimum necessary to induce them to move; if the workers need only to relocate to receive the tax break, then the employer will have to pay them the prevailing local wage.

In the latter case, this subsidy has no industrial location effects as such; it is a labor force location policy. In the former case, the wage savings accruing to the firm are an industrial relocation incentive. If the firm hires local workers as well as relocated workers (of a particular type), then the marginal wage faced by the firm is the local wage, and there is no production distortion; if the firm uses only relocated labor, then the marginal wage is less than the local wage, and there are production distortions.

A third possibility is that workers will neither relocate nor change jobs, thus forgoing the tax break. This outcome requires that the wage paid by the firm at the new site compensate workers for any added commuting costs. This could come about in one of three ways. First, the labor force at the new site might be drawn from the current locale of this firm's workers, so the market wage at the new location is already high enough to compensate for the needed travel. Second, the firm's relocation from the old site might lower the wage at that site so much that the wage at the new site becomes attractive enough to induce workers to commute from the old site to the new. Third, the firm's relocation might raise the local wage at the new site, but not enough to compensate for the added travel, so moving is still not attractive. The assumption that the firm's location decision alters market wages complicates the analysis considerably, for one then must treat input prices as nonparametric. In the absence of strong evidence to the contrary, it seems reasonable to treat each firm as small relative to the entire market.

(It should be noted that the income tax is itself an intervention in the marketplace, and therefore the market wage may not equal the marginal social cost of labor. This measurement issue lies beyond the scope of the present analysis.)

Exemption from local property taxes at the new location lowers the prices of land and improvements relative to the prices of other inputs. It can be expected to distort both location and production. As with the income tax, one must ask about possible divergences between market and social marginal costs induced by the property taxes themselves.

A *heavy tax penalty* may be imposed on those who construct new plants or expand existing facilities in areas predesignated as restricted. In Korea, the penalty is 500 percent. To the extent that this policy induces firms to locate elsewhere, it incurs only location distortions because it does not alter factor prices at the new location and the burden of the cost falls on the firm as forgone profits. To the extent that the policy fails, however, and firms either do not produce the same output or continue to build or expand in the penalized area, there will be production distortions. Whether the distortions occur in the form of reduced output or altered inputs will depend on how the assortment of income, property, and registration tax penalties cumulatively influence factor prices.

Loan guarantees for construction at the new site lower the price of capital and thereby induce both location and production distortions. Their effects are similar to those of the investment tax credit.

Special housing and consumer loans for employees of the relocated establishments have effects akin to those of the income tax break for households, although if they induce distortions in the consumer's desired consumption patterns they may not benefit the consumer dollar for dollar.

Local industrial development laws are an alternative to the above measures, all of which amount to cash grants or input price subsidies to firms. In Korea, under the Local Industrial Development Law of 1969, local industrial districts can be designated and then benefit from several government supports.

The government will pay for replotting land, for road construction, and for the development of an industrial water supply system. Further, land may be granted by the government to the developer. The provision of such services can lower the costs of firms and thereby make one site more attractive than another. As indicated above and detailed below, such in-kind subsidies to firms do not pose any special analytical problem. The gravest difficulty is empirical. It is very difficult to develop suitable measures of the availability and quality of public services and social overhead capital provided to firms by the government. Our empirical assessments of the worth of such ventures are therefore only suggestive.

One fundamental conceptual problem does emerge from this in analysis of several of the specific Korean location policies. The analysis of social cost given here assesses the cost of moving a given firm from site A to site B. The true concern of the planner is not this firm per se, however, but rather employment, or a general type of economic activity, or a specific technological process (for example, one that pollutes). Without a clear sense of what it is that planners wish to move from A to B, it is difficult to assess completely any policy. For example, a capital gains tax exemption plan is likely to draw firms that rely heavily on capital rather than labor. If employment relocation is the goal of the policy, then this measure will appeal least to some of the firms planners would most wish to move. The empirical analysis of alternative input subsidies should differentiate among industries to see if the heterogeneity of technologies across industries is sufficient to require heterogeneity in optimal industrial location policy as well.

Economic Principles

Three important economic theorems offer qualitative guidance in assessing alternative location policies. A brief summary of these theorems here will pave the way for the quantitative examination of alternative policies in the coming chapters. (For proofs of these theorems, and several generalizations of them, see appendix A.)

The first theorem says that if a policymaker is limited to

subsidizing the price of a single input to induce the firm to choose B over A, then the social cost will be minimized by subsidizing an input that is used extensively by the firm and that is poorly substituted for other inputs. The latter condition ensures that lowering the price of this input will not change much the use of other inputs from what it would otherwise be. The former condition ensures that the price of the subsidized good will not have to be lowered much to confer a subsidy large enough to counter site A's profit advantage.

To illustrate these points, consider two firms that currently use very different amounts of land but would add equal increments to the land they use if the price of land were to drop $100 per acre. To grant the same total subsidy payment to both the firms would require offering a *larger* price break (per acre) to the firm that uses less land; that firm would therefore increase its use of land more than the other and incur a larger distortion in factor usage.

Alternatively, two firms have the same initial land use, but one of them is more sensitive to changes in the price of land. The more sensitive firm will alter its factor usage more when the price of land is changed and will therefore incur a greater distortion from optimal factor usage.

The second theorem says that if a policymaker is limited to increasing the provision of one public input (for example, public transportation), then the social cost will be minimized by increasing the provision of an input for which the firm would be willing to pay much and which is a good substitute for other inputs. The former condition ensures that not much of the publicly provided good need be offered to counter the profit advantage of site A. The intuition underlying the latter condition is that it would be pointless for government to spend its money purchasing inputs for the firm if the firm were not going to reduce its expenditures—hence the desirability of providing good substitutes for the firm's inputs.

A corollary to the second theorem is that if the publicly provided input is valued more at the margin than its marginal social cost of production, then provision of that public input will enhance, not lower, economic efficiency. If the government can provide at a cost of ten dollars an input the firm values at twenty dollars (but cannot provide for itself), then there is a clear net social gain from the government's incurring the ten dollar cost.

The notion that increasing publicly provided services might lower social costs has an analog among price mechanisms as well. If market input prices do not equal the marginal social costs of those inputs, the firm's market behavior will not minimize the social costs of production. Consequently, there is room for lowering social costs by altering input prices with taxes or subsidies. The government can use its policies to ensure that the firm faces the marginal social costs of its inputs instead of the marginal market costs, and it can thereby induce the firm to minimize social costs while maximizing private profits with taxes or subsidies.

A third theorem follows from one and two: if sites A and B differ in some one factor price or some one publicly provided input, it may be better to subsidize a different factor's price or augment the provision of another service rather than close the gap between the two sites. For example, if highly skilled labor is more expensive at site B, the social cost of bringing the firm to B may be less if unskilled rather than skilled labor is subsidized. The determinants of the choice would be those given above: which kind of labor is less substitutable for other inputs, and which is used more extensively?

Another example: if roads from site B to the port city are far poorer than from site A to the port city, the social cost of bringing the firm to B might be less if the decision were to subsidize the price of highly skilled labor at site B rather than to improve the roads from B to the port city. The determination of the best policy rests on rates of substitution, the level of skilled labor utilization, and the value of better roads to the firm. This example illustrates the fact that the third theorem is in an important sense just a generalization of the first two.

This third theorem is a weaker but more general version of the economists' usual sermon. Generally (but see the corollary above) economists argue that pure cash transfers (or mandates or prohibitions) are the least costly way to achieve a policy goal. The third theorem indicates that when those kinds of "best" solutions are not politically feasible, "second-best" solutions should be sought with care. Taken together, these three theorems provide the theoretical underpinning needed to interpret the simulation results reported in chapter 3; they also focus attention on the principal relationships to be examined in the empirical work of chapter 2.

Note

1. The market prices paid for inputs by the firm reflect only the private cost of those inputs. If there are no externalities in the use of the inputs, however, and no market imperfections such as monopoly power in the sale of the inputs, then the private costs mirror the social costs of the inputs.

CHAPTER 2

The Econometric Model

THE THEOREMS DESCRIBED at the end of chapter 1 identify the important economic parameters for assessing alternative subsidy schemes: the share of costs borne by each variable input (factor shares); the marginal value to the firm of each fixed input (shadow prices); and the substitutability of each factor for others (elasticities of substitution).

The econometric model which follows uses the 1978 Korean Census of Manufacturing and the World Bank–Seoul National University Project Survey of manufacturing firms in the Seoul region to estimate the structures of technology for the nine standard industrial categories based on two-digit standard industrial codes (SICs). Examination of the factor choices of Korean firms as they face differing factor prices and differing quantities of fixed factors enabled me to estimate the elasticities of substitution among the various factors. Observation of variations in firms' costs across differing levels of fixed factors permitted me to estimate the shadow values of such inputs. Moreover, the surveys afforded direct observation of the factor shares for several variable inputs.

These data are particularly rich in information on the role of land prices in the cost structure of manufacturing firms. Few previous studies of manufacturing costs for any country have given land much attention.

It is important to keep in mind that this econometric exercise is not undertaken for its own sake. The shape and direction of the econometric investigations are dictated by the needs of the simulation model, which evaluates alternative location subsidies. The available data in many respects are far from ideal, and one may be quite skeptical about any specific numbers obtained. In the context of a simulation model, however, in which sensitivity analyses are easy to conduct, it can often suffice to use econometric tools to obtain plausible base cases from which simulation analyses can begin.

If rough econometric work can put one in the right range for parameter values, simulations can then indicate either that further econometric sophistication is uncalled for—that greater precision is not likely to alter the lessons from the exercise—or that particular parameters are of special importance and that further econometric efforts to pin down those parameters would be quite worthwhile. Where possible, we compared our econometric results with the findings of other studies of manufacturing, including studies for other developing countries and studies for the United States, using the survey reported in Reedy (1985).

The Model

An industry's technology is revealed in production activities and in the cost structures of firms. (In application, we shall use plants as the unit of analysis, but for convenience we shall refer to "firms.") By examining the relation between output and inputs (the production function) one can uncover the substitutability of factors and infer firms' optimal choices of inputs. Alternatively, by observing how firms' costs and factor choices vary with input prices, output, and levels of fixed inputs (the cost function), one can uncover the firms' optimal choices of inputs and infer the substitutability of factors.

The cost function of the firm affords elegant derivations of the principal economic theorems described in chapter 1. It also affords straightforward computations of the costs of alternative subsidy schemes. For these reasons we chose to rely on cost function specification in our empirical work.

Most generally, the cost function of the firm can be written as a function of the level of output and the prices of inputs. When some inputs are taken to be fixed (that is, not determined by the firm), the function is referred to as a "restricted cost function," and the quantities of the fixed inputs are added to the variable list. Because we wished to assess the role of publicly provided inputs in the production process, we used restricted cost functions for the Korean industries.

Theoretical exercises, such as proving the theorems of chapter 1, can use a very general specification of the restricted cost function. But for application, a concrete algebraic specification is required. Such a specification must be general enough to permit description of a wide variety of technological relationships. For example, the famous Cobb-Douglas functional form adapted to the restricted cost function problem yields

$$\frac{v}{y} = A \prod_{i=1}^{n} p_i^{a_i} \prod_{j=k+1}^{n} x_j^{b_j}$$

where v is the cost of variable inputs used; y is output; p_i are variable input prices; x_j are the quantities of the fixed inputs; and A, a_i, and b_j are parameters to be estimated. This is too restrictive for the present purposes, however, because no matter what values are allowed for A, a_i, and b_j, the elasticities of substitution among the factors are always unity, which precludes alternative degrees of substitutability among factors.

The chosen specification must, however, also be simple enough to permit straightforward calculation of the many relationships of interest, such as shadow prices and factor demands. Furthermore, the parameters of the specification must bear a well-defined relation to available empirical relationships so that reasonable, realistic values can be assigned to them in simulations.

The specification chosen here is a restricted translog cost function. The translog specification of costs has been widely used in econometric studies of production and costs.[1] Here we adapted the specification to the case of restricted cost functions. The specification is attractive because it is empirically tractable, serves as a good approximation of many alternative specifications, and offers comparability with the empirical results of other studies. The functional form used is

$$
\begin{aligned}
\ln v = b &+ \sum_{i=1}^{k} a_i \ln p_i + \sum_{i=k+1}^{n} h_i \ln q_i + d \ln y + g (\ln y) \\
&+ \frac{1}{2} \sum_{i=j}^{k} \sum_{j=1}^{k} \alpha_{ij} \ln p_i \ln p_j \\
&+ \frac{1}{2} \sum_{i=k+1}^{n} \sum_{j=k+1}^{n} B_{ij} \ln q_i \ln q_j \\
&+ \sum_{i=1}^{k} \sum_{j=k+1}^{n} \gamma_{ij} \ln p_i \ln q_j \\
&+ \sum_{i=1}^{k} \tau_i \ln p_i \ln y + \sum_{i=k+1}^{n} \theta_i \ln q_i \ln y
\end{aligned}
$$

(1)

where $\alpha_{ij} = \alpha_{ji}$ and $B_{ij} = B_{ji}$, p_i are variable input prices, q_i are fixed input quantities, y is output, and v is the cost of variable inputs used. The structural parameters to be estimated are b, a_i, h_i, g, α_{ij}, B_{ij}, γ_{ij}, τ_i, and θ_i.

Factor Shares, Shadow Prices, and Functional Restrictions

Factor shares and shadow prices, two of the key economic parameters for assessing alternative subsidy schemes, are closely related to the cost function. If raising the quantity of a fixed input by one unit lowers the costs incurred by the firm for variable factors by x dollars, the firm should be willing to pay x dollars for that unit. Hence the shadow price of a fixed input is minus the derivative of the cost function with respect to that input.

Analogously, if the price of a variable input rises by one dollar, the firm's costs will rise by the quantity of that input being used by the firm. The demand for a variable input thus is the derivative of the cost function with respect to that input price.

Taking the derivatives of both sides of the translog function with respect to the variable input prices, we get

$$S_i = \frac{p_i}{v} \frac{\partial v}{\partial P_i} = \frac{p_i q_i}{v} = a_i + \sum_{j=1}^{k} \alpha_{ij} \ln p_j$$

(2)

$$+ \sum_{j=k+1}^{n} \gamma_{ij} \ln q_i + \tau_i \ln y \qquad i = 1, \ldots, k.$$

Because $P_i q_i / v$ is the factor share for the ith factor, S_i is a factor share.

Taking the derivatives with respect to the fixed inputs yields

$$-S_i^* = \frac{q_i}{v} \frac{\partial v}{\partial q_i} = \frac{q_i w_i}{v} = h_i + \sum_{j=1}^{u} \gamma_{ij} \ln P_j$$

(3) $$+ \sum_{j=k+1}^{n} B_{ij} \ln q_i + \theta_i \ln y \qquad i = k+1, \ldots, n$$

where w_i is the shadow price of the ith input, that is, its marginal value to the firm. By analogy to S_i, S_i^* is the quasi-factor share of the ith fixed input. The expression "quasi-" is a reminder that the value of the fixed input is being set to its shadow price, which may bear no relation to what the firm pays for the input, and also that the denominator is a variable cost and does not include the shadow value of the fixed inputs.

Christensen and Greene (1976) have discussed a priori theoretical restrictions that might be placed on the parameters of an unrestricted translog cost function. If equation 1 were an *unrestricted* cost function, there would be the following restrictions:

$$\theta_i = 0, \, h_i = 0 \qquad\qquad i = k + 1, \ldots, n$$

(4) $$\gamma_{ij} = 0 \qquad\qquad i = 1, \ldots, k; \, j = k + 1, \ldots, n$$

$$B_{ij} = 0 \qquad\qquad i, j = k + 1, \ldots, n$$

That is, q_i would not appear in the equations and there would be no quasi-factor share equations.

Christensen and Greene explain that homogeneity of degree zero of factor demands in factor prices (a direct consequence of cost-minimizing behavior) would imply that *if the restrictions in 4 hold*, then

(5) $$\sum_j \alpha_{ij} = \sum_i \alpha_{ij} = \sum_i \alpha_{ij} = 0$$

Also, the fact that factor shares always sum to one requires

(6) $$\sum_{i=1}^{K} a_i = 1$$

They further note that the homotheticity of the production function underlying equation 3 requires that if the restrictions in equation 4 hold, then $\tau_i = 0$ for $i = 1, \ldots, k$, whereas the homogeneity of that production function would require $g = 0$, and linear homogeneity would add the further requirement that $d = 1$.

Because the effect of subsidies on output is not emphasized in the present study, returns to scale are less important to us than they might otherwise be. It is assumed (for convenience) that there are constant returns to scale in the production process when *all* inputs are considered. In instances in which different returns to scale seem appropriate, the simulation model can accommodate them by allowing a different technology to be set for large firms than for small firms. This limited flexibility suffices when each firm is viewed as having a fixed level of output, as is the case in this study.[2] A firm with fixed inputs will make different input choices than a firm with no fixed inputs, and it will consequently have different costs. The costs of a firm with fixed inputs are represented by a restricted cost function, not the unrestricted cost function studied by Christensen and Greene.

When there are no fixed inputs, all of Christensen and Greene's restrictions are used; in the presence of fixed inputs, however, alternative restrictions are appropriate. Using a restricted cost function (one in which the restrictions in equation 4 do not hold) does not alter the restrictions in equations 5 and 6. Factor demands are still homogeneous of degree zero in prices, and the variable factors' shares still sum to one. The remaining restrictions offered by Christensen and Greene no longer hold, however, because homotheticity in *all* factors precludes homotheticity in variable factors when some factors are fixed.

Constant returns to scale in *all* inputs require that factor shares be unchanged when factor prices remain fixed while output *and all fixed inputs* are altered equiproportionately. This restriction implies that

$$(7) \qquad \tau_i = - \sum_{j=k+1}^{n} \gamma_{ij} \qquad\qquad i = 1, \ldots, k$$

Like factor demands, shadow shares must also be homogeneous of degree zero in factor prices, so

$$(8) \qquad \sum_{j=1}^{n} \gamma_{ji} = 0 \qquad\qquad i = k+1, \ldots, n$$

Moreover, shadow shares are also unaffected by equiproportionate changes in output and fixed inputs, so

$$(9) \qquad \theta_i = - \sum_{j=k+1}^{n} B_{ij} \qquad\qquad i = k+1, \ldots, n$$

When all these restrictions on share and shadow share functions are incorporated into equation 1, it can be seen that the only remaining influence on the cost of equiproportionate changes in output and fixed inputs is through g, d, and h_i. As in the unrestricted case, the linear homogeneity of the underlying technology does require $g = 0$, but the constraint on d is modified to become

$$(10) \qquad d = 1 - \sum_{i=k+1}^{n} h_i$$

These many restrictions on the parameters of the translog restricted cost function are both a boon and a bane. They are a boon in that they reduce the amount of information required to estimate the cost structure. Given the slight variation in some variables of interest (most notably the interest rate), this parsimony is a real blessing.

When variations from the estimated cost structures are being specified for use in the simulation model, however, the restrictions become a bane in that they prevent one from simply assigning values to all the parameters and getting on with the simulation; instead, one must carefully check that all the restrictions are faithfully applied so that the resulting cost structure is consistent with an underlying technology.

Data

The primary data source for this econometric work was the Korean Census of Manufacturing for 1978. For purposes of this analysis, the key variables in the survey were: the number of production workers, wages paid to production workers, lot size, the value of the lot, the value of the structure, the value of the machinery, the value of output, the firm's two-digit industry code, and the four-digit geocode for the firm's location.

These data were supplemented by the data on interest rates (the curb rate and the bank rate) gathered by Sang-Chuel Choe of Seoul National University, by data on the rate of inflation in Korea, and by data for the two largest industries, fabricated metals and textiles, gathered in the World Bank–Seoul National University Project Survey of the Seoul region. Our discussions with government and industry officials in Korea in early 1983 confirmed that in Korea small firms generally either finance their operations internally or rely on the curb market for funds; only larger firms have access to the bank rate without special provisions by the government. This fact motivated one principal line of simulation work reported in chapter 3; it also suggested that the rental prices of assets would vary between small and large firms. Tests described below indicate that for analytical purposes it is appropriate to assume that firms below the mean size in their industry pay the curb rate, whereas larger firms pay the bank rate.

Deciding what interest rates firms pay is a special case of a more general problem: the proper measurement of prices in the cost function. Output is produced and costs are incurred by the firm anew in each period; both output and costs thus are flow concepts. Similarly, labor is hired anew each period; labor services also are a flow concept. Capital and land, conversely, persist from period to period; they are stock concepts. To properly account for the role of land and capital in the firm's cost structure requires converting capital and land values to their rental values.

We chose our units of measure for capital so that the purchase price of capital is unity. Consequently, the rental price of capital is the real interest rate plus the rate of depreciation. A 6 percent rate of depreciation is assumed in the pricing of capital. Exploratory analysis indicated that other depreciation rates over a modest range would not much alter our empirical results.

Because the purchase price of land varies by geocode, the rental price of land will also vary by geocode. We chose our units of measure for land so that the purchase price was unity in Seoul center city. This implies that at that location the rental price of land was the real interest rate.

We first tried to estimate the price of land by dividing reported lot value by reported lot size. Unfortunately, we found unbelievable variances in the price of land computed this way. We hypothesized that firm managers who answered the survey questions were unclear about either their lot values or their lot sizes and consequently gave error-ridden answers to these questions. This hypothesis suggested that better estimates of the price of land could be obtained by computing the mean reported price of land in each four-digit geocode area, a speculation that proved quite accurate.[3] For this reason, we present only results based on the geocode means for land prices.

Our findings regarding the land price variable, derived directly from reported lot value and lot size, led us to try two measures of land value in computing firms' costs. First, we used reported land value; second, we used reported lot size times mean land price over the firm's four-digit geocode. Our results are not very sensitive to which measure we look at.

The labor data provided by firms seem much more precise than the land data. Within industries, within geocodes, the variation in reported wage rates (production workers' wages divided by the number of production workers) was relatively much smaller than that in reported land prices. We believe this was the result of better knowledge on the part of managers about how many employees they have and what they pay them than about the size of their lot or its market worth. This is not unreasonable when one realizes that the former numbers are almost constantly subject to the manager's discretion whereas lot size is only infrequently altered and hence its price is of less pressing interest.

The geographic variation observed in land prices is considerable, but less than has been observed in many other cities. There is a twentyfold difference between land prices in central Seoul and those on the outskirts of the province; a fiftyfold difference is more common. In wage rates, however, there is a much less pronounced pattern by geocode. Although there does seem to be a relation between wage rates and locations, it is very slight, possibly because of the dampening effects of commuting to and from the city center using transit provided by the firm.

In addition to using the geocode-specific mean price for land, we relied on geocode-specific means for other variables to provide instruments for use in two-stage least squares estimations that we conducted. The rationale for this was that the behavior of firms within a geocode was likely to be correlated, but that the individual peculiarities (the disturbance terms) of one firm would not be reflected in the behavior of its neighbors. Because we take factor prices and publicly provided inputs (and their proxies) as independent of the firm, the instrument's only role is to purge a quantity of any bias because of the endogeneity rooted in the quantity's relation to costs and factor shares. Since the two-stage least squares analyses did not appreciably differ from the ordinary least squares results, we report only the latter.

In addition to using land, labor, and capital as the firms' inputs, we toyed with using office workers as well as production workers as an additional labor category. However, both missing data and a high degree of multicolinearity between the two wage rates ultimately led us to reject this idea.

In our efforts to measure the effects of publicly provided inputs, we examined the proportion of a geocode's area devoted to streets, the proximity of the geocode to a highway, the electricity transmission capacity in the geocode, and the distance of the geocode from the central business district (an inverse proxy for accessibility). As will be seen below, the results of this exercise were for the most part disappointing. As a consequence, for the simulation models we had to resort to the use of proxies to obtain parameters for publicly provided inputs.

Estimation

Equations 1, 2, and 3 all contain the parameters of our econometric model. If we treat these equations jointly and impose the constraints on the parameters above, we arrive at a general strategy for estimating our restricted translog cost function. In practice, however, we made no use of equation 3 because the shadow shares were unobserved.

At this juncture our preoccupation with the simulation model begins to shape the empirical work. The share equations 2 and 3 suffice to estimate Y_{ij} and α_{ij}, which are sufficient (coupled with factor shares) to compute the substitution relationships among variable factors and between the variable and fixed factors. The cost function itself has the potential for augmenting the information drawn from equation 2 in three ways. First, more efficient estimates of γ_{ij} and α_{ij} might be obtained. Second, the cost function offers information about returns to scale. Third, estimates could be obtained of B_{ij}, which inform us about the price elasticities of demand that would apply to the fixed factors if they were to become variable rather than fixed.

Initial estimates from the two largest industries, however, indicated that none of the advantages from focusing on equation 1 were forthcoming. When equation 1 was coupled with equation 2, we learned:

- The theoretical constraints on the parameters implicit in their repeated appearances across the equations are not rejected in the data at hand.
- The parameter estimates of α_{ij} and γ_{ij} from equation 2 alone are nearly identical to those obtained from equations 1 and 2 taken together.
- B_{ij} cannot be estimated at all precisely with the data at hand; the standard errors on these parameters were always large.

On the basis of these preliminary findings, we chose to rely on equation 2 to estimate the elasticities that were of interest in studying each of the nine manufacturing industries in detail.

Estimation of the parameters of equation 2 is straightforward but mechanically cumbersome. Note that each α_{ij} appears in two share equations, that for input i and for input j. Also recall that the share equations must always sum to one.

The adding-up property implies that once $k - 1$ shares are estimated, the kth is known, so one share equation is dropped in the estimation procedure. (The empirical results are unaffected by which share equation is dropped.) The repetition of the α_{ij}s across equations can be handled by physically "stacking" the equations—and the data—so that the equations are estimated by least squares procedures as if they were a single equation.

In stacked form, for example, the variable attached to coefficient α_{ij} would be $\ln P_j$ if the dependent variable were input i, and $\ln P_i$ if the dependent variable were input j. For coefficients appearing in only one equation, a similar treatment applies. For example, the variable attached to γ_{ij} would be $\ln q_j$ if the dependent variable were input i but would be a zero otherwise.

Ordinary least squares (OLS) applied to such stacked equations yield maximum likelihood estimates of the parameters of the model under the usual OLS conditions. Instrumental variable estimators can also be applied to such stacked equations to obtain consistent parameter estimates under the usual conditions.

Summary of Estimation Results

Before reporting the results of a series of hypothesis tests, it is important to emphasize once again the relationship between the econometric model and the simulation model. The data base used in this study is a rich one and has the potential to permit subtle distinctions to be made among alternative hypotheses. Indeed, with large sample sizes such as ours (ranging from 580 to 3,418) one must expect that the data will expose the fact that the translog specification is at best only an approximation of the true cost function. Many specific hypotheses about the model are likely to be rejected for this reason alone. Our real concern, however, is not whether α_{ij}, say, is 0.01 or 0.011; rather, our concern is with differences in parameter values that are large enough to matter in the application of the simulation model. In this regard we find the model to be quite robust with respect to alternative sets of restrictions on the parameter values.

On the one hand, we found that when small firms were assumed to pay the curb interest rate and large firms the bank rate, the technologies estimated for the two groups were quite similar, although we could generally reject the hypothesis of identical technologies at the 10 percent level. (Small firms were defined to be firms below the mean level of output for the industry, and large firms were those above the mean level. Fiddling with the break point had no appreciable effect on our results.) Restricting large and small firms to pay identical interest rates, on the other hand, led to much more sharply distinguishable estimates of the cost function.

When we combine the data from the large and small firms, more often than not we do not reject the hypothesis that all the theoretical restrictions implied by cost minimization hold. Even in the cases in which the constraints are rejected, the rejection is mild. This suggests that the translog is a reasonably good approximation of the true underlying cost minimization function. Similarly, conditional on the above restrictions, we generally fail to reject the hypothesis of constant returns to scale in all inputs.

The coefficients of the price variables are uniformly significant. The fixed input variables perform much less satisfactorily, however. The electricity, highway, and streets variables are each significant in fewer than 10 percent of the cases. Only the distance measure is persistently significant. The distance measure reveals a persistent pattern of substituting away from labor and toward capital and land as accessibility declines, a result in accord with our intuitions.

Tables 1 and 2 contain the estimates of α_{ij} and γ_{ij} from the translog cost share equations with all restrictions imposed. Land value is measured as reported lot size times the mean price of land for the four-digit geocode area. Tables 3 and 4 contain the estimates with land value measured by the land value reported by the firm. The parameters estimated directly appear with t-statistics; the parameters derived from the estimated parameters using the parameter restrictions appear without t-statistics.

Table 5 presents mean elasticities of substitution from the models reported in tables 1 through 4 evaluated at the mean factor shares for each of the nine industries (see appendix B for the elasticity formulas). A limitation of the translog specification is that it permits concave regions in the isoquants of the

Table 1. Own and Cross-Price Interaction Terms (α_{ij})
in the Translog Restricted Cost Function by Industry

Input	Land	Labor	Capital	Land	Labor	Capital
		Food			Textiles	
Land	0.09	−0.06	−0.03	0.12	−0.07	−0.05
	(8.90)[a]	(−8.47)		(9.13)	(−7.95)	
Labor	−0.06	0.08	−0.02	−0.07	0.12	−0.05
		(7.50)			(10.61)	
Capital	−0.03	−0.02	0.05	−0.05	−0.05	0.10
		Wood			Paper	
Land	0.12	−0.07	−0.05	0.04	−0.06	0.02
	(9.13)	(−7.95)		(3.73)	(−8.04)	
Labor	−0.07	0.12	−0.05	−0.06	0.10	−0.04
		(10.61)			(9.25)	
Capital	−0.05	−0.05	0.10	0.02	−0.04	0.02
		Chemicals			Minerals	
Land	0.08	−0.04	−0.04	0.17	−0.07	−0.10
	(7.40)	(−7.07)		(9.32)	(−7.13)	
Labor	−0.04	0.10	−0.06	−0.07	0.08	−0.01
		(13.68)			(6.18)	
Capital	−0.04	−0.06	0.10	−0.10	−0.01	0.11
		Basic metals			Fabricated metals	
Land	0.10	−0.03	−0.07	0.07	−0.04	−0.03
	(5.83)	(−3.33)		(9.73)	(−9.74)	
Labor	−0.03	0.11	−0.08	−0.04	0.11	−0.07
		(8.05)			(20.93)	
Capital	−0.07	−0.08	0.15	−0.03	−0.07	0.10
		Other				
Land	0.05	−0.04	−0.01			
	(3.30)	(−4.39)				
Labor	−0.04	0.11	−0.07			
		(8.96)				
Capital	−0.01	−0.07	0.08			

a. Expressions in parentheses are *t*-statistics.

underlying technology. In the simulation model we modify the translog so that elasticities of substitution never become negative but rather stay constant at zero once they reach zero. For this reason, we simply report the estimated negative elasticities as the zeros they become in the simulation model.

Reedy (1985) surveys econometric estimates of elasticities of substitution in the United States and in developing countries. That survey provides a useful benchmark to assess the plausibility of the elasticity estimates in table 5. Table 6 reports the median elasticity of substitution found by Reedy for each indus-

Table 2. Price and Fixed-Input Interaction Terms (Y_{ij}) in the Translog Restricted Cost Function by Industry

Input	Distance	Electricity	Highway	Streets	Distance	Electricity	Highway	Streets
	Food				*Textiles*			
Land	0.045	0.009	0.003	-0.045	0.020	-0.001	0.008	-0.017
	(3.79)[a]	(1.00)	(0.43)	(-2.49)	(2.60)	(-0.33)	(1.68)	(-1.46)
Labor	-0.051	-0.014	0.001	0.039	-0.025	-0.005	-0.002	0.003
	(-4.32)	(-2.74)	(0.11)	(2.25)	(-3.35)	(-1.87)	(-0.037)	(0.23)
Capital	0.006	0.005	-0.004	0.006	0.003	0.004	-0.009	0.016
	Wood				*Paper*			
Land	0.045	0.001	0.018	-0.039	0.011	-0.007	0.001	-0.013
	(3.20)	(0.16)	(1.70)	(-1.84)	(0.72)	(-1.19)	(0.13)	(-0.62)
Labor	-0.048	-0.005	-0.009	0.023	-0.058	0.008	0.013	0.034
	(-3.41)	(-0.86)	(-0.92)	(1.12)	(-4.14)	(1.29)	(1.31)	(1.67)
Capital	0.003	0.004	-0.009	0.016	0.047	-0.001	-0.014	-0.021
	Chemicals				*Minerals*			
Land	0.051	-0.003	0.017	-0.007	0.085	-0.026	0.016	-0.009
	(4.18)	(0.67)	(2.40)	(0.49)	(4.16)	(3.46)	(1.51)	(-0.35)
Labor	-0.059	0.005	-0.006	-0.008	-0.073	0.011	-0.016	-0.003
	(5.06)	(1.29)	(-0.93)	(-0.56)	(-3.65)	(1.60)	(-0.55)	(-0.14)
Capital	0.008	-0.002	-0.011	-0.015	-0.012	0.015	—	0.012

Input	Distance	Electricity	Highway	Streets	Distance	Electricity	Highway	Streets
	Basic metals				*Fabricated metals*			
Land	0.020	−0.005	−0.003	−0.029	0.035	−0.002	0.003	−0.021
	(0.93)	(−0.83)	(−0.22)	(1.12)	(4.35)	(−0.63)	(0.63)	(−1.93)
Labor	−0.048	−0.003	0.022	0.046	−0.048	−0.005	0.004	0.021
	(2.26)	(−0.48)	(1.65)	(1.84)	(−6.06)	(−1.55)	(0.87)	(2.01)
Capital	0.028	0.008	−0.019	−0.017	0.013	0.007	−0.007	—
	Other							
Land	0.033	0.002	−0.001	−0.016				
	(1.81)	(0.32)	(−0.096)	(−0.58)				
Labor	−0.055	−0.011	−0.002	0.038				
	(−3.14)	(−0.62)	(−0.21)	(1.47)				
Capital	0.022	0.009	0.003	−0.022				

a. Expressions in parentheses are *t*-statistics.

31

Table 3. Alternative Own and Cross-Price Interaction Terms (α_{ij}) in the Translog Restricted Cost Function by Industry

Input	Land	Labor	Capital	Land	Labor	Capital
		Food			*Textiles*	
Land	0.06	−0.06	0.002	0.05	−0.04	−0.01
	(4.92)[a]	(−7.34)		(6.41)	(−7.98)	
Labor	−0.06	0.12	−0.06	−0.04	0.12	−0.08
		(9.79)			(14.75)	
Capital	0.002	−0.06	0.06	−0.01	−0.08	0.09
		Wood			*Paper*	
Land	0.06	−0.07	0.01	0.03	−0.06	0.03
	(3.06)	(−5.61)		(2.15)	(−6.98)	
Labor	−0.07	0.17	−0.10	−0.06	0.12	−0.06
		(9.94)			(9.50)	
Capital	0.01	−0.10	0.09	0.03	−0.06	0.03
		Chemicals			*Minerals*	
Land	0.04	−0.05	0.01	0.13	−0.07	−0.06
	(2.77)	(6.74)		(8.54)	(7.62)	
Labor	−0.05	0.13	−0.08	−0.07	0.09	−0.02
		(14.59)			(8.15)	
Capital	0.01	−0.08	0.07	−0.06	−0.02	0.08
		Basic metals			*Fabricated metals*	
Land	0.02	−0.03	0.01	0.04	−0.05	0.01
	(1.23)	(−2.49)		(4.55)	(−9.65)	
Labor	−0.03	0.13	−0.10	−0.05	0.13	−0.08
Capital	0.01	−0.10	0.09	−0.01	−0.08	0.07
		Other				
Land	0.05	−0.04	−0.01			
	(2.43)	(−3.60)				
Labor	−0.04	0.13	−0.09			
		(8.55)				
Capital	−0.01	−0.09	0.10			

a. Expressions in parentheses are *t*-statistics.

try for the United States and for developing economies. (In computing the medians, studies of specific members of an industry—for example, glass companies within the minerals industry—were excluded since it is unclear how estimates for more narrowly defined firms relate to the industrywide elasticities.)

Comparison of tables 5 and 6 reveals that our estimates are persistently somewhat lower than the medians of other studies. All our values are well within the middle range of numbers reported by others, however. One reason for caution in comparing our results with Reedy's is that the studies she reports for specific industries are generally two input production functions, labor and capital, whereas our results rely on three inputs. To check for the sensitivity of our results to this difference, we also estimated translog restricted cost functions for the three inputs taken in pairs.

Table 7 reports the resulting elasticities of substitution. On the whole, the elasticities of substitution between labor and capital reported in table 7 conform more closely to those in table 5 than to those in table 6. This suggests that the differences in our results are not rooted in our multifactor specification but either reflect a genuine difference in Korean technology from that used elsewhere or are rooted in statistical quirks of the models and data used by ourselves and others.

Because few other studies have included land among the factors used by manufacturing firms, we have no checks within the literature for our elasticities of land with other factors. By using the World Bank–Seoul National University Survey of 500 firms in the Seoul region, however, we were able to obtain independent estimates of these elasticities for the two largest industry groups, textiles and fabricated metals. The results of this analysis are reported in table 8. The elasticities for capital and labor and for land and labor are higher than from the larger Korean survey; those for capital and labor are in the range found in the Reedy survey. The elasticities for land and capital, however, are lower than those from the larger Korean survey.

The main lesson we draw from tables 5–8 is that the potential for variability in estimates of elasticities of substitution is modest but genuine and that our simulations should reflect this potential by permitting variation in elasticities of substitution for all factors within the ranges reported in tables 5–8. We also note with some satisfaction that when land and capital are focused on in isolation, the elasticities of substitution we estimate are positive in all cases. Moreover, those elasticities are lowest, and generally quite low, in those cases in which the multifactor translog obtained negative elasticities of substitution between land and capital when evaluated at mean factor shares. This is quite in accord with our decision in the simulation model below to impose zero elasticities when negative elasticities are estimated. Further, it underlies our choice to use very low but nonzero values for the elasticity of substitution when establishing *initial* values in the industries with negative estimates. (This assumption simply assures us that in their

Table 4. Alternative Price and Fixed-Input Interaction Terms (Y_{ij}) in the Translog Restricted Cost Function by Industry

Input	Distance	Electricity	Highway	Streets	Distance	Electricity	Highway	Streets
	Food				*Textiles*			
Land	-0.001	0.002	-0.019	-0.036	0.009	-0.010	0.005	0.015
	(-0.04)[a]	(0.38)	(-2.35)	(-1.73)	(1.01)	(-2.87)	(0.93)	(1.10)
Labor	-0.023	-0.004	0.021	0.060	-0.022	0.011	-0.001	-0.012
	(-1.69)	(-0.65)	(2.52)	(2.94)	(-2.54)	(3.37)	(-0.15)	(-0.89)
Capital	0.024	0.002	-0.002	-0.024	0.003	-0.002	0.018	-0.017
	Wood				*Paper*			
Land	0.026	-0.010	-0.038	-0.012	-0.001	-0.006	-0.004	0.015
	(1.30)	(-1.11)	(-2.51)	(-0.41)	(-0.07)	(-0.82)	(-0.36)	(0.63)
Labor	-0.029	0.012	0.020	0.029	-0.044	0.007	-0.006	0.013
	(-1.42)	(1.38*)	(1.38*)	(0.98)	(-3.42)	(1.10)	(1.21)	(1.14)
Capital	0.003	-0.002	0.018	-0.017	0.0565	-0.002	-0.010	-0.041
	Chemicals				*Minerals*			
Land	0.016	0.003	0.012	-0.00003	0.064	-0.019	0.009	-0.002
	(-0.07)	(-0.82)	(-0.36)	(0.63)	(1.19)	(0.71)	(1.50)	(-0.0016)
Labor	-0.054	0.008	0.014	0.026	-0.044	0.007	-0.006	0.013
	(-3.42)	(1.10)	(1.21)	(1.14)	(-3.74)	(1.83)	(-1.41)	(-0.05)
Capital	0.005	-0.002	-0.010	-0.041	0.028	-0.010	-0.006	-0.01297

Input	Distance	Electricity	Highway	Streets	Distance	Electricity	Highway	Streets
	Basic metals				*Fabricated metals*			
Land	−0.028	0.002	−0.012	−0.033	0.012	0.001	−0.004	−0.017
	(−1.17)	(0.28)	(−0.75)	(−1.16)	(1.26)	(0.31)	(−0.06)	(−1.31)
Labor	−0.004	0.003	0.011	0.072	−0.053	−0.011	−0.0002	0.046
	(−0.17)	(0.45)	(0.74)	(2.59)	(−3.97)	(−0.96)	(0.93)	(2.99)
Capital	0.032	−0.005	0.001	−0.039	0.026	0.002	−0.0056	−0.020
	Other							
Land	0.032	0.004	−0.002	−0.021				
	(1.57)	(0.48)	(−0.20)	(−0.71)				
Labor	−0.053	−0.011	−0.0002	0.046				
	(−2.70)	(−1.44)	(−0.02)	(1.56)				
Capital	0.021	0.007	0.0022	−0.025				

a. Expressions in parentheses are *t*-statistics.

Table 5. Elasticities of Substitution among Variable Inputs

Industry	Land-labor	Land-capital	Capital-labor
Food	0.23	0.76	0.76
Textiles	0.42	0.51	0.54
Wood	0.40	0.41	0.37
Paper	0.38	0.66	0.59
Chemicals	*	1.45	0.71
Minerals	0.34	*	0.86
Basic metals	0.54	*	0.44
Fabricated metals	0.32	0.52	0.55
Other	0.34	0.57	0.43

*Indicates negative estimated elasticity. Hence, zero is a better estimate.

Table 6. Median Elasticities of Substitution between
Capital and Labor in Reedy's Survey of U.S.
and Developing-Country Studies

Manufacturing industry	United States	Developing countries
Food	0.75	0.80
Textiles	0.85	0.59
Wood	0.85	0.89
Paper	0.96[a]	1.00[b]
Chemicals	0.83[c]	0.88
Minerals	0.98	0.75
Basic metals	0.81	0.86
Fabricated metals	0.72	0.92
Other	1.10[d]	0.81

a. Paper 1.06, printing 0.86.
b. Paper 1.17, printing 0.87.
c. Chemicals 0.89, petroleum 0.78, rubber 0.82.
d. There were only two studies for the manufacturing sector as a whole.

Table 7. Elasticities of Substitution from Two
Variable-Factor Translog Restricted Cost Functions

Industry	Land-labor	Land-capital	Capital-labor
Food	0.42	0.46	0.74
Textiles	0.53	0.45	0.67
Wood	0.35	0.13	0.54
Paper	0.34	0.65	0.69
Chemicals	0.62	0.41	0.62
Minerals	0.55	0.12	1.15
Base metals	0.33	0.18	0.35
Fabricated metals	0.46	0.29	0.57
Other	0.50	0.40	0.43

Table 8. Elasticities of Substitution in Korean Manufacturing Using an Alternative Survey of Manufacturing Firms

Industry	Land-labor	Land-capital	Capital-labor
Textiles	0.61	0.27	0.72
Fabricated metals	0.57	0.14	0.77

initial position firms are not operating along nonstrictly convex portions of their isoquants; it permits government policies to move firms to the cusps of the isoquants and indeed assures that initially these particular firms are near the cusp.)

Publicly Provided Inputs

The most disappointing aspect of the econometric results is the weak performance of the variables intended to reflect publicly provided inputs. Several interpretations of these results bear mentioning.

First, it is possible that the publicly provided inputs we examined do not substitute for land, labor, or capital either at all or sufficiently for the tradeoff to be measurable. That would leave open the question whether the inputs are substitutes for other inputs or simply sine qua non for the production of certain goods, without which firms do not operate. Nonsubstitution between public and private inputs will not exclude them altogether, but will limit the number and sizes of firms in an area to the extent that the publicly provided inputs are not public goods. For example, electricity transmission capacity is a good from which users can be excluded and that cannot be inexhaustibly consumed by as many users as want to use it.

An implication of this interpretation is that the volume of output from a particular location might be the only aspect of industry behavior influenced by public investments. If such is the case, studying the effects of location policy on quantities produced by firms becomes markedly more important than recognized in the simulations. Furthermore, the relationships among publicly provided inputs in supporting private production also become important because the goal of government would be to find the least costly configuration of public inputs that could support a given level of output. Such a study would be quite separate from an analysis of private inputs if there is little or no substitution among public and private factors.

Second, it might be that publicly provided inputs substitute to an appreciable degree only for inputs that are not included in the present study, chiefly materials and energy. It is difficult to imagine that publicly provided inputs substitute *only* for materials or energy, but it is possible that the subactivities the firm would have to engage in to replace publicly provided inputs would, at the margin, be highly energy-intensive. For example, a firm with trucks might impress the trucks for transit duty at the start and end of the day with little incremental capital costs, and hence the gasoline costs might loom large in the balance.

Third, it may be that although the publicly provided inputs found at any one site are exogenous to the firm, the firm chooses a location precisely because the resources available there are superior to those of other locations. This would make the fixed inputs truly variable (within a set restricted by local opportunities) for the firm. Such simultaneity of fixed inputs and variable input choices could lead to biases in our parameter estimates that mask the true relationships between variable and fixed inputs.

Fourth, the data at hand may be too coarse to permit extraction of the true underlying relationships. The data on firms are from 1978; the data on publicly provided inputs are from 1983. This five-year lag in data may cover up the true relationships between the variable and fixed inputs.

Fifth, one might imagine that it was too ambitious to include all the publicly provided inputs in the function, that multicolinearity among them would drown them all. We reject this possibility because specifications in which only subsets of the public inputs were included led to no improvement in the performances of any of them. The only finding from these runs was a hint of *positive* correlations between electricity capacity and the use of capital and labor. Such a finding is quite consistent with the endogeneity interpretation given above.

Sixth, one might take the results at their face value. Perhaps no one publicly provided input has enough effect to be uncovered (just as one might be hard pressed to analyze a small subset of the work force in a study such as this), whereas the *collection* of publicly provided inputs still does have an appreciable effect on factor choices. Moreover, perhaps the overall level of public support for firms is closely enough correlated with distance from the city center for distance to serve as a proxy capable of reflecting the influence of publicly provided inputs as a whole.

Given the structure of our model and the poor performance of other measures of publicly supplied inputs, we are left with little choice but to accept for now this last, optimistic, interpretation of our results. The gravest limitation to treating distance from the city center as a proxy for infrastructure is that centralized location is also correlated with other production advantages such as proximity to customers and inputs.

The simulation model relies on the elasticities of variable factor demands with respect to fixed factors. Because in our exploration of the influences of fixed inputs we estimated these parameters directly using log-linear factor demand equations (to see if the poor performance of those variables was rooted in the restrictions of the translog specification), it is preferable when specifying the simulation model to rely on those estimates for the elasticities of variable input demands with respect to the distance function. This judgment rests on two considerations. The first is the heavy computational burden of using the translog parameters to compute these elasticities which, as is demonstrated in appendix B, depend on the unobserved shadow shares of the fixed inputs. Second, and more important, the double-log specification yields elasticity estimates that are robust with respect to the relationship between fixed inputs and output. If fixed inputs are available equally for the production of each unit of output, the effective level of such inputs is proportional to output. At the other extreme, fixed inputs are available equally to each firm independently of output, and the effective level of such inputs is independent of output. The log specification yields the same elasticity with respect to fixed inputs in either case; only the interpretation of the output coefficient differs between the two. This robustness makes these elasticity estimates especially useful in the simulations.

Table 9 contains the elasticities of interest for each industry. The parameter estimates were relatively insensitive to the use of OLS or two-stage least squares, as well as to the inclusion or exclusion of other measures of public inputs. It is worth noting that the log-linear factor demand equations gave further support to the assumption of the linear homogeneity of the

Table 9. Demand Elasticities of Variable Inputs with Respect to Distance from the City Center by Industry

Industry	Land	Labor	Capital
Food	0.41 (3.6)[a]	0.05 (0.7)	0.30 (2.4)
Textiles	0.41 (6.1)	0.16 (3.3)	0.29 (4.7)
Wood	0.38 (2.7)	−0.11 (1.0)	0.03 (0.2)
Paper	−0.09 (0.2)	0.16 (0.7)	0.56 (1.7)
Chemicals	0.46 (4.5)	−0.04 (0.7)	0.21 (2.2)
Minerals	0.72 (3.2)	−0.06 (0.6)	0.41 (2.4)
Basic metals	0.35 (1.5)	0.09 (0.6)	0.57 (2.7)
Fabricated metals	0.50 (6.2)	0.06 (1.5)	0.23 (3.4)
Other	0.66 (3.1)	0.69 (3.6)	0.16 (0.6)

a. Figures in parentheses are t-statistics.

underlying technology because all but a few of the income coefficients were not significantly different from unity.

Notes

1. See Christensen and Greene (1976) for an early cost function application.

2. In retrospect, I regret having laid aside output effects. I chose to do so because the empirical work indicates constant returns to scale in manufacturing, so the distortions per unit of output are constant for all policies. Nonetheless, because the subsidies reduce marginal costs, sometimes substantially, the output consequences of location policies are probably greater than I originally thought.

3. Regressions of the log of land used by firms against the log of the prices of land as computed from the individual firm's responses to the survey frequently gave insignificant coefficients on the price of land. The same regressions using the mean price of land by geocode, however, repeatedly yielded significant land price coefficients of the appropriate sign. These relative performances of the two price measures were mirrored in their performances in other factor demand equations as well.

We wondered if perhaps the firm-specific data, although not as rich as the geocode means, might still contain information not found in the geocode means. To test this notion we tried instrumental variable estimators based on these two variables. The instrumental variable estimators were generally in the neighborhood of the estimates obtained with the geocode means in ordinary least squares (OLS) estimators. This result is consistent with the notion that all the relevant information about the price of land is to be found in the geocode means.

CHAPTER 3

Simulating Alternative
Policies

THE THEORETICAL AND ECONOMETRIC ANALYSES of the previous chapters provide a foundation for quantifying the costs and benefits of alternative schemes for subsidizing Korean manufacturing. A principal advantage of using simulation models in conjunction with econometric studies of technology is that one can explore the robustness of one's findings through sensitivity analyses. Moreover, rather than simply quantifying existing circumstances, simulations enable one to ask "what if" questions. Proposed policy schemes can be compared with current schemes to judge the efficiency of the present policies and to suggest how they might be improved.

Simulation Model

To influence a firm's location decision, the government must offer a subsidy that overcomes the cost or profit disadvantage of the site it favors. No matter what input is subsidized, and no matter whether the subsidy results in a lower price or a larger quantity, the subsidy must lower the firm's cost by some specific amount.

The computer program for the simulation model offers two ways to specify the benefit required to move the firm. First, one can enter into the program a particular cost reduction that all subsidies must provide. The program will then calculate what price reduction would result from a given variable input, what quantity increase would result from a given variable input, or what quantity increase for a given input that is otherwise fixed is needed to provide the firm the required benefits. Second, one can specify that a particular price reduction or quantity increase be given the firm; the program then will calculate the cost reduction the firm would realize.

The cost of input subsidies to the government is generally

larger than the benefits of such subsidies to the recipients. The difference between the cost of a subsidy and its benefit to a firm is the deadweight loss that results from the distortions in incentives for the firm created by the subsidy. A central function of the simulation model is to calculate the deadweight loss for each potential subsidy plan. If each of several subsidies offers a firm the same level of benefits, the most efficient is the one with the smallest deadweight loss.

The simulation model assumes that a firm's variable costs fit the restricted translog function described in chapter 2. For a particular subsidy scheme, the model uses the cost function and the share equations to compute the firm's costs and factor demands with and without the subsidy. By comparing the firm's unsubsidized costs with, in turn, its subsidized costs and the full market value of the resources it would use under the subsidy, the program obtains the benefits and deadweight loss that would result from the subsidy. (Appendix A explains in detail the benefits, deadweight losses, and efficiency of alternative subsidy schemes.)

The simulation model has a more difficult task when the input provided is a benefit level that a subsidy must offer. The program first discovers an upper bound for the subsidy and then conducts a binary search over possible values of the subsidy to determine the amount of the chosen input that yields the required benefits to the firm. Once the subsidy scheme is ascertained, the program computes benefits, subsidized factor demands, and deadweight loss according to the same logic.

An important practical problem in calculating deadweight losses is that the marginal *social* values of the inputs usually are the appropriate prices to use in computing them. In the absence of externalities, government intervention, and imperfect competition, it is common to rely on market prices to reflect marginal social values. But there are no market-determined prices for publicly provided inputs to use as a proxy for their marginal social values.

One obvious proxy for the marginal social value of a publicly provided input would be an estimate of its marginal cost to the government. Such a cost-based value would probably be as acceptable as a market price if it were not for the shared nature of so many publicly provided inputs. Many firms benefit from improved road service to the urban center from some fringe business zone, for example, and consequently an appropriate allocation of cost across the beneficiaries must reflect this sharing. It unfortunately is not easy to guess the appropriate fraction of marginal social cost to charge each firm in assessing the deadweight loss (or gains) associated with changes in fixed, publicly provided inputs.

Luckily, this problem does not arise in discussing subsidies for variable inputs. For them there are acceptable proxy values for social costs. Such subsidies also involve no changes in fixed inputs and hence no need to compute changes in the value of fixed inputs from unsubsidized to subsidized conditions. (In the one instance in which there are serious questions about appropriate marginal social prices for variable inputs—interest rates—there are well-defined alternatives that permit the cases to be analyzed sensibly.) But there are some serious dilemmas in considering subsidies to fixed inputs. In these cases we have developed three competing measures of deadweight loss (or indicators of inefficiency) that may help evaluate these particularly nettlesome policies.

First, deadweight loss is assessed using both the method described above and a user-provided guess at the initial social price of the fixed input. Second, deadweight loss is assessed on the assumption that the unsubsidized shadow price of the fixed factor is the true social price of the input. Third, it is reported how the initially declared social value would have to change if the deadweight loss from the subsidy were zero.

The simulation model's final chores are to summarize the percentage changes in factor prices and quantities associated with the subsidy scheme in question and to express the deadweight loss as fractions of benefits to the firm, total subsidy costs, and the firm's output. One limitation of the model is that subsidy schemes are presumed to influence input mix but not output levels. It would be worthwhile in follow-up research to adapt the model to permit output effects. To assess correctly the inefficiencies associated with output changes would, however, require estimates of the market demands for manufactured goods, a task beyond the scope of this research.

(Appendix D contains the documented Fortran code for the twenty subroutines that comprise the simulation model. Appendix B describes the theoretical relationships that enable the program to parameterize the translog restricted variable cost function from elasticities and factor shares provided by the user.)

Determining the Parameters of the Model

The first step in conducting simulations is determining what cases are of interest. In the present study this determination has two dimensions: the technologies to be analyzed and the policies to be studied.

The ranges of factor share combinations and technological substitution relations examined in this section are intended to be representative of the Korean manufacturing sector. The classification scheme used by the manufacturing survey that underlies the econometric work reported in chapter 2 divided the manufacturing sector into nine primary categories: food, textiles, wood, paper, chemicals, minerals, basic metals, fabricated metals, and "others." (The largest two of these nine industries are textiles and fabricated metals.) Policies are simulated for each of the nine industries.

The factors of production emphasized here are labor, capital, and land. None of the subsidy plans in use in Korea subsidizes material inputs, so they are not included in the analysis. Labor is the single largest remaining component of firm costs for all industries; capital is generally the next largest component. Capital and land, as is shown below, are the inputs for which government subsidies are most important in Korea.

Mean annual costs for labor, land, and capital for firms in the nine manufacturing industries range from about 75 million to 145 million won a year according to the survey data. To facilitate comparisons across simulations, however, the industries are lumped into two cost categories. The lower cost category includes the wood, chemicals, and "other" industries and has a typical annual cost level of 100 million won. The higher cost category includes the remaining industries and has a typical annual cost level of 125 million won.

The mean annual values of output in manufacturing are much higher than the mean annual costs of land, labor, and capital. This reflects the importance of factors of production that are not included in this analysis, such as materials, energy, and entrepreneurial risk-taking. The variance in mean annual output values across industries is considerably greater than that in mean annual land, labor, and capital costs.

Table 10 reports typical output levels for small, medium-sized, and large firms in each of the nine industries. These figures correspond approximately to the means of output levels

Table 10.   Annual Output of Firms of Various Sizes
by Industry
(millions of won)

Industry	Firm size		
	Small[a]	Medium[b]	Large[c]
Food	150	2,250	18,000
Textiles	100	800	3,000
Wood	75	475	2,500
Paper	150	900	2,600
Chemicals	200	1,400	6,500
Minerals	100	625	2,000
Basic metals	300	1,550	8,500
Fabricated metals	200	1,200	6,500
Other	150	475	1,400

a. Approximately the mean of all firms in the industry group whose output is below
the mean output for the industry as a whole.

b. Approximately the mean output for the industry for all firms analyzed.

c. Approximately the mean of all firms in the industry whose output is above the
mean output for the industry as a whole.

for all firms in the 1978 Korean Census of Manufacturing, for
firms below that industry mean, and for firms above that industry mean.

The shares of land, labor, and capital in annual costs vary
appreciably across industries. The mean share of land ranges
from about 8 to 20 percent; that for capital from about 20 to
40 percent; and that for labor from about 45 to 70 percent.

The computation of factor shares requires that assumptions
be made about the real rate of interest borne by firms for funds
tied up in land and capital. Altering one's assumptions about
that interest rate could alter the share of labor relative to those
of land and capital, but the pattern of factor share differences
across industries would be little affected. As is discussed below,
it is plausible to believe that the shares reported here give lower
bounds for mean shares of labor and upper bounds for mean
shares of land and capital.

To facilitate comparisons across simulations, factor shares are
rounded in the cases analyzed below; the results are relatively
insensitive to this rounding. Table 11 reports the typical factor
shares for each industry that are used in the simulations.

The econometric work of others and that reported in chapter
2 yield estimates of the elasticities of substitution among land,

Table 11.   Typical Factor Shares by Industry

| | | Factor | |
Industry	Land	Labor	Capital
Food	0.15	0.45	0.40
Textiles	0.10	0.65	0.25
Wood	0.20	0.60	0.20
Paper	0.10	0.60	0.30
Chemicals	0.15	0.55	0.30
Minerals	0.20	0.60	0.20
Basic metals	0.15	0.60	0.25
Fabricated metals	0.10	0.65	0.25
Other	0.10	0.70	0.20

Table 12.   Typical Elasticities of Substitution among
Land, Labor, and Capital by Industry

Industry	Land-labor	Land-capital	Capital-labor
Food	0.25	0.75	0.85
Textiles	0.40	0.50	0.85
Wood	0.40	0.40	0.85
Paper	0.10	1.45	1.00
Chemicals	0.40	0.65	0.85
Minerals	0.35	0.10	1.00
Basic metals	0.55	0.10	0.85
Fabricated metals	0.30	0.50	1.00
Other	0.35	0.60	1.50

labor, and capital for each of the manufacturing industries. On
the basis of these estimates, the values found in table 12 were
established for these elasticities. Rounding again was used to
achieve easier comparability across simulations, although the
results are relatively insensitive to the rounding.

   The empirical evidence for the elasticities of demand for land,
labor, and capital with respect to publicly provided inputs is not
at all precise. There is a strong negative correlation, however,
between distance from the city center and publicly provided
infrastructure. Lee, Choe, and Pahk (forthcoming) used the
World Bank–Seoul National University survey to tally firms'
assessments of the quality of various public services in the Seoul
region. Table 13 is taken from their report. They used five circu-
lar zones going out from the center of the city (ring 1 includes
the central business district) to examine the quality of six

publicly provided services. As is clear from the table, the perceived quality of services declines steadily as the distance from the city center increases. Estimates of the elasticities of the demand for land, labor, and capital with respect to publicly provided infrastructure that exploit the strong negative correlation between distance from the city center and publicly provided infrastructure are reported in table 14. As proxies for the elasticities with respect to infrastructure, elasticities with respect to distance from the CBD were obtained for manufacturing firms in the 1978 Korean Census of Manufacturing. These numbers provide at least useful initial values for analyses involving publicly provided inputs.

Table 13. Quality of Urban Infrastructure Provisions by Zone in the Seoul Region
(percentage of establishments in each zone)

	Zone					
Provision	1	2	3	4	5	All
Electricity never interrupted	67	57	58	35	28	47
Water never interrupted	71	85	83	49	15	61
Excellent telephone service	100	76	53	46	58	56
Excellent telegraph service	71	41	14	25	5	26
Excellent garbage collection[a]	19	11	10	7	10	9
Excellent fire protection	57	58	39	25	35	36
Number of establishments	21	85	112	241	40	499

a. There were 178 firms that responded as using garbage collection.
Source: Lee, Choe, and Pahk (forthcoming).

Table 14. Base Values for Elasticity of Demand for Privately Purchased Inputs with Respect to Publicly Provided Inputs

Industry	Land	Labor	Capital
Food	−0.40	−0.05	−0.30
Textiles	−0.40	−0.15	−0.30
Wood	−0.40	−0.05	−0.05
Paper	−0.05	−0.15	−0.55
Chemicals	−0.40	−0.05	−0.20
Minerals	−0.70	−0.05	−0.40
Basic metals	−0.40	−0.10	−0.60
Fabricated metals	−0.50	−0.05	−0.25
Other	−0.70	−0.70	−0.15

Note: Based on elasticities with respect to distance from city center.

Simulation Scenarios

The second determination to be made in conducting simulations is which subsidies should be addressed. The World Bank–Seoul National University Project Survey provides strong evidence that attention should be focused on credit subsidies and land price subsidies. Of the 141 firms in the survey that had relocated, 50 reported credit subsidies as the most important government subsidy available to them (8 more cited credit subsidies as somewhat important), and 15 reported subsidized land prices as most important (32 more cited land price subsidies as somewhat important). No other subsidy was cited by more than 4 firms as most important. Nonetheless, the large factor share of wages suggests that wage subsidies may be an efficient alternative to land or credit subsidies; hence wage subsidies deserve some attention in the following analyses.

In addition to the subsidy programs that offer benefits to individual firms, the government has undertaken large investments in urban infrastructure that may influence firms' location decisions. For example, the government has created a new industrial city, Banwoel, located 40 kilometers southwest of downtown Seoul. The government has provided roads, housing, structures, electricity, water, sewerage, and municipal services in Banwoel in the hope of attracting firms to locate there. Although an evaluation of a complex plan such as that for Banwoel is beyond the scope of our model, it is worthwhile to explore as best we can with our model the efficiency of public infrastructure investments.

Credit subsidies are sometimes tied to capital loans and are sometimes allowed on loans used to purchase either land or capital. When the credit subsidy is tied to capital loans, it amounts to a reduction in the price of capital. As noted in chapter 1, investment tax credits also provide a reduction in the price of capital. Consequently, when credit subsidies tied to capital are analyzed below, comparably valued investment tax credits implicitly are also being analyzed. Such tax credits were cited by 14 of the 141 firms as somewhat important.

Chapter 1 also noted that property tax exemptions were equivalent to land price subsidies for analytical purposes. Thirty-three firms in the World Bank–Seoul National University Survey cited property taxes as somewhat important.

Apart from credit and land price subsidies, the subsidies most cited by firms as somewhat important were programs that introduce no production distortion: tax breaks on relocation expenses or capital gains on old plant and equipment (29 firms), exemption from registration and acquisition taxes (34 firms), and tax breaks on cash relocation grants (21 firms). But a measure of the quantitative importance of these programs is that even taken together they are cited as most important by only 11 firms. Credit and land price subsidies are clearly the programs that deserve particular attention.

Loan guarantees are the most common form of credit subsidy in Korea. These guarantees raise complex questions about the proper measurement of the market price of capital for subsidized firms that must be addressed to properly analyze the efficiency of these subsidies.

The following sections analyze credit subsidies (emphasizing loan guarantees), land price subsidies, and the provision of public infrastructure. The chapter closes with a discussion of firm size.

Simulating Loan Guarantees

The loan guarantee simulations that follow overlook fixed factors and restrict attention to land, labor, and capital. The loan guarantees analyzed are those sometimes given to firms that relocate according to government wishes. Many firms moving to the new industrial city of Banwoel, for example, received such subsidies.

A curiosity about these guarantees is that they do not offer lower interest rates than ordinary bank loans. They only guarantee access. Since the large firms in each industry generally can get access to bank loans these guarantees attract only small and medium-sized enterprises that would otherwise be unable to obtain loans.

Firms unable to obtain bank credit must rely on either the curb market or internal financing. Since in our travels in the Seoul region we repeatedly were told by firm managers that curb market financing with rates about double those of banks was prohibitively expensive for their enterprises, we conclude that the real curb interest rate provides an upper bound on the opportunity cost of capital to the firm shut out from bank financing. Consequently, on the supposition that the curb rate is the true opportunity cost of capital for firms receiving guarantees, analysis of the benefits and deadweight loss of loan guarantees provides upper bounds on both the benefits to the firms and the extent of deadweight losses.

Curb Interest Rate versus Bank Interest Rate

Table 15 presents the simulated benefits and deadweight losses from loan guarantees that lower the real interest rate faced by the firm from the curb rate to the bank rate for two cases: (1) the loans can be used for land or capital expenditures and (2) the guaranteed loans can be used only for capital expenditures. Most of the loan guarantees offered by the Korean government appear to be of the capital-only variety. Some firms, however,

Table 15. Benefits and Deadweight Losses from Lowering the Interest Rate from the Curb Rate to the Bank Rate

Industry	Benefits[a] (B)	Deadweight loss[a] (D)	B ÷ cost[b]	B ÷ (B + D)
	Subsidizing land and capital loans			
Food	58.33	13.84	0.467	0.808
Textiles	40.18	13.92	0.321	0.743
Wood	37.12	9.75	0.371	0.792
Paper	44.58	16.42	0.357	0.731
Chemicals	40.44	11.80	0.404	0.774
Minerals	46.73	13.22	0.374	0.779
Basic metals	47.21	16.31	0.378	0.743
Fabricated metals	40.87	16.32	0.327	0.715
Other	31.88	18.75	0.319	0.630
	Subsidizing capital loans only			
Food	43.46	17.25	0.348	0.716
Textiles	28.63	13.75	0.229	0.676
Wood	18.13	8.22	0.181	0.688
Paper	36.86	21.87	0.295	0.628
Chemicals	26.99	12.20	0.270	0.689
Minerals	23.06	11.22	0.184	0.673
Basic metals	27.42	10.96	0.219	0.714
Fabricated metals	30.14	17.14	0.241	0.637
Other	23.44	20.31	0.234	0.536

Note: The curb interest rate is taken as the marginal social cost of a loan.

a. Millions of won a year.

b. Cost is 125 million won a year for all industries except wood, chemicals, and other. For those three industries, costs are 100 million won a year. (See text for discussion.)

do receive unrestricted loan guarantees, so both types are examined.

Table 15 reveals that general loan guarantees are most attractive to industries with low labor cost shares, such as the food industry, and least attractive to industries with high labor cost shares, such as the other industry group. As expected, loans only for capital are more attractive to industries with high capital shares (see table 11): food, paper, and chemicals.

Within an industry, deadweight losses will rise as benefits rise since greater benefits require greater distortions in prices. Deadweight losses do not uniformly rise with benefit levels across industries, however, because of differences in the cost functions across industries. For a striking example, deadweight losses are greater in the industry least favored by general loan guarantees (the "other" industry group) than in the most favored industry (the food industry).

Loan Guarantees versus Alternative Subsidies

Rather than offering firms loan guarantees, the government could offer subsidies on other inputs that would be equally valued by the firm. As noted above, land price subsidies are frequently used by the government. The large cost share of wages suggests that wage bill (price of labor) subsidies also should be considered. But would such alternative schemes be more or less efficient than loan guarantees? Since the value of the interest subsidy depends on whether loans are for land and capital or for capital alone (see table 15 for the differences), alternative policies must be examined at two different levels of generosity in these comparisons.

The simulation model conducts these analyses by beginning with the benefit levels given in table 15 from the interest rate reduction schemes. The computer program then calculates how deep a subsidy on another input's price (for example, the price of land) would yield the firm those same benefits. The value of all inputs chosen by the firm under the new subsidy scheme is then compared with the lowest cost at which the firm could produce its output given market prices. The difference is the deadweight loss associated with the subsidy scheme.

Table 16 compares the loan guarantees with several alternative subsidy mechanisms that yield equal benefits to the firms. Subsidies only on the price of land, only on the price of labor,

Table 16. Comparison of Loan Subsidies with Equally Valued Subsidies on Other Inputs when the Loan Subsidy Drops Interest Rate from the Curb Rate to the Bank Rate

Subsidy	Food	Textiles	Wood	Paper	Chemicals	Minerals	Basic metals	Fabricated metals	Other
	Efficiencies[a] *of land and capital loan subsidy*								
Loan	0.808	0.743[b]	0.792[b]	0.731[b]	0.774[b]	0.779[b]	0.743[b]	0.715[b]	0.630[b]
Land	0.958[b,c]	0.981[b,c]	0.967[b,c]	0.936[b,c]	0.950[b,c]	0.991[b,c]	0.975[b,c]	0.992[b,c]	0.985[b,c]
Labor	0.663	0.912	0.877	0.869	0.818	0.870	0.862	0.904	0.909
Capital	0.577	0.518	0.330[b]	0.550	0.487	0.273	0.436	0.502	0.427
	Efficiencies[a] *of capital-only loan subsidy*								
Loan	0.716	0.676	0.688	0.628	0.689	0.673	0.714	0.637	0.536
Land	0.944[b,c]	0.973[b,c]	0.935[b,c]	0.924[b,c]	0.927[b,c]	0.983[b,c]	0.957[b,c]	0.989[b,c]	0.980[b,c]
Labor	0.786	0.944	0.954	0.899	0.897	0.950	0.933	0.936	0.937

a. Efficiency = benefits ÷ (benefits + deadweight loss).
b. The subsidized input demand (land if several inputs are subsidized) became perfectly inelastic at a price above the subsidized price.
c. The subsidy required a negative price on the subsidized input.

and only on the price of capital are reported (the restricted loan guarantee is itself a subsidy only on the price of capital, so that comparison is not given). Since each subsidy scheme matches the unrestricted or restricted loan guarantee in benefits, the only differences are in the efficiencies of the subsidy mechanisms, which are measured as the ratio of firms' benefits to the social cost (benefits plus deadweight loss) of the subsidy. The interest rate subsidy rows in table 16 are the efficiencies reported in table 15. The remaining rows are the corresponding efficiencies (benefits divided by the sum of benefits and deadweight loss) for the alternative subsidy plans.

In general, direct subsidies to land or labor are more efficient than unrestricted loan guarantees, whereas subsidies on capital's price alone are markedly less efficient. The roots of these differences are not all the same. Land price subsidies are particularly efficient primarily because of the relatively low elasticity of substitution of land for other inputs. Labor price subsidies appear to derive most of their advantage from having a higher cost share than capital. In the one industry (food) with a higher cost share for capital than for labor, the labor subsidy is *less* efficient than the unrestricted loan guarantee.

The unrestricted loan guarantee subsidies are large enough to require quite large subsidies of only land or only capital if the benefits from the unrestricted loan guarantees are to be matched. Indeed, in most instances one would have to put a negative price on land to match the guarantee. Needless to say, such a strategy would be politically untenable. Since this difficulty may be an artifact of using the curb rate, which is only an upper bound on the true opportunity cost of credit, alternative cases are examined below. Even at this most generous level, however, subsidies to labor costs appear a viable and more efficient alternative to interest subsidies.

Guarantees for loans on capital alone are less efficient than land or labor subsidies yielding equal benefits to the firm. Given the greater efficiencies of land or labor subsidies relative to capital subsidies as alternatives to unrestricted guarantees, this result is not surprising. It is somewhat surprising, however, that capital-only loan guarantees are always 10 percent or so less efficient than unrestricted loan guarantees, despite the fact that the unrestricted guarantees offer benefits to the firms roughly half again as large.

The explanation for this seeming anomaly is that the subsidy to land that differentiates the restricted and unrestricted loan guarantees is highly efficient, which raises the overall efficiency of the unrestricted guarantees above that of the restricted guarantees. The root of this efficiency is that as the price of land falls markedly (as it does under the unrestricted guarantee plan), most firms virtually run out of opportunities for substituting land for labor and capital. When the elasticity of substitution between land and other factors falls to zero, further subsidization of land results in no additional deadweight loss. This effect leads to a high average efficiency for large subsidies to the price of land.

Half the Curb Rate versus the Bank Rate and Alternatives Revisited

The curb rate provides an upper bound on the opportunity cost of capital to small and medium-sized firms. Perhaps a better guess of the true opportunity cost would be the midpoint between the bank and curb rates of interest. Tables 17 and 18 are patterned after tables 15 and 16 but are based on the assumption that typical small and medium-sized firms face an interest rate halfway between the bank and curb rates. Table 17 makes clear why so many firms cite credit subsidies as very important. The benefits from either unrestricted or capital-only loan guarantees are very high relative to the firms' costs.

Comparisons between tables 16 and 18 confirm the rather general result that *within* industries the degree of inefficiency associated with a specific type of subsidy declines with the generosity of the subsidy. The only exceptions are land subsidy alternatives, the efficiency of which, as explained above, rises once possibilities for substitution are exhausted.

The lesser subsidies in tables 17 and 18 are not enough lower than those in tables 15 and 16 to make land subsidies a viable alternative, despite their attractively high efficiency. The share of land in total costs is so small that the government would in general have to pay firms for the land they use to match the benefits of loan guarantees.

Furthermore, the reduced generosity closes the gap somewhat between unrestricted loan guarantees and subsidies to labor costs, although the latter are still generally preferable—and clearly dominate capital-only loan guarantees. Similarly, the gap between capital-only and unrestricted loan guarantees is

Table 17. Benefits and Deadweight Losses from Lowering the Interest Rate to the Bank Rate from Half the Sum of the Bank and Curb Rates

Industry	Benefits[a] (B)	Deadweight loss[a] (D)	B ÷ cost[b]	B ÷ (B + D)
	Subsidizing land and capital loans			
Food	43.98	5.66	0.352	0.886
Textiles	29.79	5.73	0.238	0.839
Wood	28.95	4.54	0.290	0.865
Paper	32.94	5.45	0.263	0.858
Chemicals	30.67	5.46	0.307	0.849
Minerals	33.04	5.47	0.288	0.868
Basic metals	35.62	7.61	0.285	0.824
Fabricated metals	29.92	6.20	0.239	0.828
Other	22.59	6.86	0.226	0.828
	Subsidizing capital loans only			
Food	29.85	6.02	0.239	0.832
Textiles	19.61	5.26	0.157	0.788
Wood	12.48	3.22	0.125	0.795
Paper	24.67	8.17	0.197	0.751
Chemicals	18.60	4.69	0.186	0.799
Minerals	15.77	4.32	0.126	0.785
Basic metals	19.08	4.36	0.153	0.814
Fabricated metals	20.28	6.39	0.162	0.761
Other	14.81	7.21	0.148	0.673

Note: Half the sum of the bank and curb rates is taken as the marginal social cost of a loan.

a. Millions of won a year.

b. The cost is 125 million won a year for all industries except wood, chemicals, and other. For those three industries, the costs are 100 million won a year. (See text for discussion.)

narrowed somewhat, though the former are still markedly less efficient despite their lesser benefits.

Loan Guarantees and Inefficient Credit Rationing

There is an alternative perspective on loan guarantees. The above analyses assumed that the true marginal cost of credit to small and medium-sized firms is the curb rate or some other rate above the bank rate. In this view, allowing these firms access to bank credit rates distorts true factor prices and induces inefficiencies in operations. But it is more plausible to

Table 18. Comparison of Subsidies with Equally Valued Subsidies on Other Inputs when Loan Subsidy Drops Interest Rate to Bank Rate from Half the Sum of the Bank and Curb Rates

Subsidy	Food	Textiles	Wood	Paper	Chemicals	Minerals	Basic metals	Fabricated metals	Other
Efficiencies[a] of land and capital loan subsidy									
Loan	0.886[b]	0.839[b]	0.865[b]	0.858[b]	0.849	0.868[b]	0.824[b]	0.828[b]	0.767[b]
Land	0.988[b,c]	0.974[b,c]	0.958[b,c]	0.916[b,c]	0.936[b,c]	0.989[b,c]	0.967[b,c]	0.989[b,c]	0.979[b,c]
Labor	0.782	0.941	0.915	0.913	0.878	0.911	0.907	0.936	0.939
Capital	0.722	0.660	0.461	0.667	0.637	0.456	0.604	0.640	0.548
Efficiencies[a] of capital-only loan subsidy									
Loan	0.832	0.788	0.795	0.751	0.799	0.785	0.814	0.761	0.673
Land	0.983[b,c]	0.962[c]	0.914	0.891[b,c]	0.898[c]	0.975[c]	0.940[c]	0.985[b,c]	0.968[b,c]
Labor	0.871	0.964	0.970	0.939	0.936	0.968	0.957	0.960	0.962

a. Efficiency = benefits − (benefits + deadweight loss).
b. The subsidized input demand (land if several inputs are subsidized) became perfectly inelastic at a price above the subsidized price.
c. The subsidy required a negative price on the subsidized input.

argue that small and medium-sized firms face an artificial barrier to bank borrowing and that the true marginal cost of credit to these firms is the bank rate, not the curb rate. If this alternative view is correct, as seems likely, small and medium-sized firms suffer increased costs and society suffers deadweight losses from the artificial credit prices faced by these firms in the curb market or elsewhere.

Tables 19 and 20 report the cost increases and the deadweight losses suffered from artificial credit constraints imposed on typical firms in each industry, as well as what those deadweight losses would be if only land were affected (that is, under

Table 19. Cost Increases and Deadweight Losses from Artificially High Interest Rates on Land and Capital Loans or Capital-Only Loans, Given that the Artificial Rate is the Curb Rate

Industry	Increased costs[a]	Deadweight loss[a]	Percentage cost increase[b]	Deadweight loss as fraction of initial cost (L)	L_1-L_2
		High interest on land and capital			
				L_1	
Food	58.33	8.34	0.875	0.125	
Textiles	40.18	8.27	0.474	0.098	
Wood	37.12	6.42	0.590	0.102	
Paper	44.58	8.43	0.554	0.105	
Chemicals	40.44	7.23	0.679	0.121	
Minerals	46.77	8.36	0.597	0.107	
Basic metals	47.21	9.95	0.607	0.128	
Fabricated metals	40.87	8.96	0.486	0.106	
Other	31.88	9.74	0.468	0.143	
		High interest on land only			
				L_2	
Food	14.87	3.21	0.223	0.048	0.077
Textiles	11.55	2.13	0.136	0.025	0.073
Wood	18.99	3.06	0.302	0.049	0.053
Paper	7.72	1.33	0.096	0.017	0.088
Chemicals	13.84	2.95	0.226	0.050	0.071
Minerals	23.67	2.65	0.302	0.034	0.073
Basic metals	19.79	4.06	0.254	0.052	0.076
Fabricated metals	10.74	1.47	0.128	0.017	0.089
Other	8.43	1.29	0.124	0.019	0.124

a. Millions of won a year.
b. The initial cost is what costs would be at the bank rate of interest.

Table 20. Cost Increases and Deadweight Losses
from Artificially High Interest Rates on Land
and Capital Loans or Capital-Only Loans Given that the
Artificial Rate Is Half the Sum of the Bank and Curb Rates

Industry	Increased costs[a]	Deadweight loss[a]	Percentage cost increase[b]	Deadweight loss as fraction of initial cost (L)	L_1–L_2
	High interest on land and capital				
				L_1	
Food	43.98	4.27	0.543	0.053	
Textiles	29.79	4.39	0.313	0.046	
Wood	28.95	3.71	0.407	0.052	
Paper	32.94	4.32	0.358	0.047	
Chemicals	30.67	4.03	0.442	0.058	
Minerals	36.04	4.50	0.405	0.051	
Basic metals	35.62	5.54	0.399	0.062	
Fabricated metals	29.92	4.51	0.315	0.047	
Other	22.59	4.83	0.292	0.062	
	High interest on land only				
				L_2	
Food	13.95	2.56	0.172	0.032	0.021
Textiles	10.18	1.59	0.107	0.017	0.029
Wood	16.47	2.24	0.232	0.032	0.020
Paper	8.27	1.49	0.090	0.016	0.031
Chemicals	12.07	2.24	0.174	0.032	0.036
Minerals	20.27	1.81	0.228	0.020	0.031
Basic metals	16.54	2.73	0.185	0.031	0.031
Fabricated metals	9.64	1.10	0.101	0.012	0.035
Other	7.77	1.03	0.100	0.013	0.049

a. Millions of won a year.
b. The initial cost is what costs would be at the bank rate of interest.

capital-only loan guarantees). Table 19 is premised on firms'
paying the curb rate when denied bank financing. Table 20 is
premised on their paying a rate halfway between the bank and
curb rates.

The first column of tables 19 and 20 reports the increase in
costs incurred by typical firms when the interest rate rises artificially from the bank rate. The second column reports the deadweight losses induced by these artificially high interest rates.
The third column expresses that deadweight loss as a function
of costs in the absence of the artificially high interest rates. The
fourth column reports the decline in deadweight loss (expressed

as a fraction of costs in the absence of artificially high interest rates) if firms were given capital-only loan guarantees and thus faced the artificially high interest rate only on loans for land purchases.

The most important numbers in tables 19 and 20 are the figures for deadweight loss. The higher credit costs paid by small and medium-sized manufacturing firms are after all income to someone else and therefore not a real loss to the Korean economy. By contrast, the deadweight losses are real subtractions from the general economic welfare.

The average deadweight loss in table 19 is approximately 11–12 percent of land, labor, and capital costs; that in table 11 approximately 5 percent. Since the small and medium-sized firms that are affected by credit restrictions account for as much as 40 percent of all manufacturing production (based on estimates from the 1978 Korean Census of Manufacturing), the numbers in table 19 translate roughly into a 4.5 percent increase in land, labor, and capital costs for all manufacturing as a result of the credit restrictions. The comparable figure from table 20 is 2.0 percent. These figures presume that it is the bank rate that reflects the true marginal cost of credit to small and medium-sized firms in Korea.

The numbers in tables 19 and 20 suggest two important lessons for Korean policymakers. First, artificial credit restrictions on the manufacturing sector do not come cheaply; the 2–4 percent of all manufacturing costs for land, labor, and capital is an appreciable social cost to be incurred from such policies. Second, given the presence of such credit restrictions, their relaxation is a promising approach to subsidizing firms as part of industrial relocation programs.

A third lesson worth drawing from tables 19 and 20 is that restricted loan guarantees that offer access only to capital loans realize the greater part of the available windfalls. Such restricted access schemes could reduce the deadweight losses associated with credit restrictions by about two-thirds.

There is an important lesson to be found in comparing tables 15 and 17 with tables 19 and 20. Measuring the effect of loan guarantees on social welfare depends critically on which view of the true marginal cost of credit to small and medium-sized firms is correct. Juggling elasticities of substitution and factor shares—for example, as is done here across industries—has relatively little effect on an assessment of the relative benefits and efficiencies of alternative policies. But shifting one's view about which interest rate is appropriately taken as the true marginal cost of credit drastically alters the balance between benefits and deadweight losses.

In table 15, for example, the efficiency of unrestricted guarantees ranges from 0.63 to 0.81 across industries, a spread of 0.18. For unrestricted loan guarantees, however, the spreads *within* industries between the efficiencies in table 15 and those implicit in table 19 average about 0.50. (For example, from table 19, a restricted loan guarantee to a typical food industry firm would lower the firm's costs by 58.33 while at the same time *reducing* deadweight loss by 8.34. Thus the efficiency measure applied to table 19 yields an efficiency of 1.17, or 0.37 higher than reported in table 15.)

The point is made perhaps more forcefully another way: If the true social cost of loans to small and medium-sized firms is the curb rate or some other rate above the bank rate, subsidies to capital are the *least* efficient mechanisms for industrial relocation; but if the true social cost is the bank rate, capital subsidies are the *most* efficient mechanisms for industrial relocation.

Low Elasticities of Substitution

Tables 15–20 are based on the elasticities of substitution given in table 12. The capital-labor elasticities given are those of the majority view in the study of Korean manufacturing discussed in chapter 2, studies of U.S. manufacturing, and studies of manufacturing in developing countries surveyed by Reedy (1985).

In five instances, however, a minority view of the capital-labor elasticity was sharply below the majority one. Usually the lower value arose from the specific study of Korean data described in chapter 2 (see tables 5 and 7). Consequently, it is of interest to see how the findings of tables 15–20 are affected by using markedly lower capital-labor elasticities in those five industries. Table 21 reports the alternative capital-labor elasticities used.

Tables 22, 23, and 24 are derived in the same fashion as tables 17, 18, and 20 except that the elasticities of substitution between capital and labor are set at the alternative, lower values. (Replications of tables 15, 16, and 19 lead to qualitative results similar to those shown in tables 22, 23, and 24, so they are not reported.)

Table 21. Alternative Capital-Labor Elasticities of Substitution

Industry	Capital-labor
Textiles	0.55
Wood	0.40
Basic metals	0.45
Fabricated metals	0.55
Other	0.45

Table 22. Results from Table 17 Using Alternative (Lower) Capital-Labor Elasticity

Industry	Benefits[a] (B)	Deadweight loss[a] (D)	B ÷ cost[b]	B ÷ (B + D)
		Capital and land		
Textiles	28.58	3.76	0.229	0.984
Wood	27.95	2.98	0.279	0.904
Basic metals	34.22	5.50	0.274	0.861
Fabricated metals	28.09	3.17	0.225	0.899
Other	19.57	1.82	0.196	0.915
		Capital only		
Textiles	18.27	2.96	0.146	0.861
Wood	11.24	1.02	0.112	0.817
Basic metals	17.42	1.47	0.139	0.922
Fabricated metals	18.27	2.96	0.146	0.861
Other	11.50	1.48	0.115	0.886

a. Millions of won a year.

b. The cost is 125 million won a year for all industries except wood, chemicals, and other. For those three industries, the costs are 100 million won a year. (See text for discussion.)

The lower elasticities of substitution between capital and labor bring a very slight decline in the differences between firms' costs under high and low interest rates. More substantial effects are seen when deadweight losses are examined.

As shown in table 22, the efficiency of unrestricted loan guarantees rises some, especially for the other industry group (in which the largest elasticity change is made, from 1.5 to 0.45), if one takes the nonbank rate as the marginal social cost. The efficiency of capital-only loan guarantees goes up markedly, as would be expected since capital is the good that has become less substitutable for other inputs.

But table 23 shows that increased efficiency of subsidized

Table 23. Results from Table 18 Using Alternative (Lower) Capital-Labor Elasticity

Subsidy	Textiles	Wood	Basic metals	Fabricated metals	Other
	Efficiencies of land and capital subsidy[a]				
Loan	0.884	0.904[b]	0.861	0.899[b]	0.915[b]
Land	0.973[b,c]	0.957[b,c]	0.966[b,c]	0.988[b,c]	0.976[b,c]
Labor	0.957	0.941	0.934	0.960	0.976
Capital	0.771	0.957[b]	0.948[b]	0.775	0.880[b]
	Efficiencies of capital-only subsidy[a]				
Loan	0.861	0.917	0.922	0.861	0.886
Land	0.959[b,c]	0.917	0.935[b]	0.982[b,c]	0.959[b]
Labor	0.976	0.982	0.973	0.977	0.988

a. Efficiency = benefits − (benefits + deadweight loss).

b. The subsidized input demand (land if several inputs are subsidized) became perfectly inelastic at a price above the subsidized price.

c. The subsidy required a negative price on the subsidized input.

Table 24. Results from Table 20 Using Alternative (Lower) Capital-Labor Elasticity

Industry	Increased costs[a]	Deadweight loss[a]	Percentage cost increase[h]	Deadweight loss as fraction of initial cost (L)	L_1-L_2
	Land and capital				
				L_1	
Textiles	28.58	3.17	0.296	0.033	
Wood	27.95	2.71	0.388	0.038	
Basic metals	34.22	4.14	0.377	0.046	
Fabricated metals	28.09	2.69	0.290	0.028	
Other	19.57	1.82	0.243	0.023	
	Capital only				
Textiles	10.31	1.61	0.107	0.017	0.016
Wood	16.70	2.28	0.232	0.032	0.006
Basic metals	16.80	2.77	0.185	0.031	0.015
Fabricated metals	9.82	1.12	0.101	0.012	0.016
Other	8.08	1.07	0.100	0.013	0.010

a. Millions of won a year.

b. The initial cost is what costs would be at the bank rate of interest.

loans for capital expenses does not qualitatively alter the relative merits of subsidies on land, labor, and capital. Labor subsidies still tend to be the most efficient, with land subsidies slightly dominant over capital subsidies. The quantitative differences between land and capital subsidies, however, cause doubt that there is any good reason for choosing one over the other on the grounds of efficiency.

The lower elasticities of substitution also lower the simulated deadweight losses associated with artificially raising the cost of credit from the bank rate to a higher nonbank rate. In table 20, a 2 percent increase in the resource cost of land, labor, and capital in Korean manufacturing arose from such a policy. In table 24, the comparable figure is 1.5 percent, with an especially large drop in the "other" industry group.

Nonetheless, 1.5 percent of manufacturing costs for land, labor, and capital is not a trivial amount, and the deadweight losses recorded in tables 22 and 23 are also nontrivial. Consequently, even if the substitution between labor and capital is at the lower end of what might be expected, differences in the efficiencies of alternative subsidy mechanisms should not be overlooked.

Using the alternative, lower elasticity measures for the substitutability of labor and capital has not altered comparisons among alternative policies. Therefore, in the following simulation exercises the higher, "dominant" views on these elasticities are relied on.

Simulating Land Price Subsidies

Land price subsidies are the second most important relocation policy, according to firm managers. Most of these subsidies in the Seoul region are offered to firms that move to the new industrial city of Banwoel. The absence of private land markets makes it difficult to assess the degree of these subsidies. But private discussions with local developers and assessments by firm managers (obtained in a small informal survey conducted by S. C. Choe of Seoul National University) suggest that in 1985 the market value of land in Banwoel was about a half to a third the price in Seoul. Firms located in Banwoel actually paid only a fourth or a fifth of the market value.

The following analysis of publicly providing infrastructure as

Table 25. Benefits and Deadweight Loss from 75 Percent Land Subsidies Given High and Low Elasticities of Demand for Variable Inputs with Respect to Fixed Inputs

	High elasticity specification				Low elasticity specification			
Industry	Benefits[a] (B)	Deadweight loss[a] (D)	B ÷ costs	B ÷ (B + D)	Benefits[a] (B)	Deadweight loss[a] (D)	B ÷ costs	B ÷ (B + D)
Food	20.92	6.04	0.166	0.776	22.85	7.21	0.174	0.760
Textiles	13.83	2.80	0.114	0.831	15.11	3.51	0.118	0.811
Wood	22.21	3.55	0.207	0.862	24.33	4.90	0.221	0.832
Paper	16.16	7.60	0.135	0.680	16.25	7.27	0.128	0.691
Chemicals	16.71	4.64	0.162	0.782	18.27	5.73	0.172	0.761
Minerals	24.09	1.26	0.191	0.950	28.33	2.31	0.212	0.924
Basic metals	24.75	6.17	0.179	0.800	22.75	5.29	0.174	0.811
Fabricated metals	13.10	1.27	0.105	0.912	14.69	1.96	0.114	0.882
Other	9.57	1.88	0.117	0.835	11.29	21.41	0.120	0.824

a. Millions of won a year.

a policy alternative to subsidizing land prices relies on a restricted cost function that includes land, labor, and capital as variable inputs and (as explained above) an inverse distance from the center of Seoul as a proxy for public infrastructure. At 2 kilometers from the center of Seoul, the price of land is at the upper end of what anecdotal evidence suggests is the price range for Banwoel. If the price of land varies to reflect differences in publicly provided infrastructure, the level of such infrastructure in Banwoel would be somewhat below that found 2 kilometers from the center of Seoul. Yet because land 2 kilometers from the center also benefits from better accessibility[1] and greater privately provided infrastructure (such as agglomeration effects), the level of publicly provided inputs in Banwoel must be somewhat higher than its land price would suggest. For this reason public infrastructure in Banwoel is assumed to equal that found 2 kilometers from the center of Seoul.

Because of our uncertainty about the elasticities between publicly provided and variable inputs, we conducted our analyses using both the elasticities reported in table 14 and also elasticities equal to half those values (with the exception that elasticities equal to 0.05 were not further reduced). The estimated elasticities capture the cost savings associated with better publicly provided infrastructure, better privately provided infrastructure (such as agglomeration effects), and better accessibility found closer to the city center. Since public policies cannot alter all these items, the sensitivity of factor demands to publicly provided inputs is probably less than the elasticities of table 14. This is the rationale for examining the lower elasticities.

The benefits and deadweight losses from a 75 percent land price subsidy for typical firms in each manufacturing industry are presented in table 25. This subsidized land price, the market land price, and the level of public infrastructure are all chosen with the intent of mimicking the land price subsidies offered firms in Banwoel. The table makes it obvious why so many firms find the land price subsidies important. The cost reductions realized by the firms range from 10 to 20 percent of the firms' expenditures on land, labor, and capital (see the third and seventh columns of table 25). This is a generous level of benefits comparable to the benefits from capital-only loan guarantees reported in table 17—although well below the benefits from unrestricted loan guarantees. The efficiency of these land price

Table 26. Efficiencies of Land, Labor, and Capital Price Subsidies Yielding Benefits Equal to 75 Percent Land Price Subsidy

Price subsidized	Food	Textiles	Wood	Paper	Chemicals	Minerals	Basic metals	Fabricated metals	Other
					Efficiencies of high elasticity[a] specification				
Land	0.776	0.831	0.862[b]	0.680	0.782	0.950[b]	0.800	0.912[b]	0.835[b]
Labor	0.917	0.975	0.939	0.960	0.944	0.948	0.942	0.975	0.962
Capital	0.871	0.839	0.620	0.808	0.815	0.589	0.756	0.833	0.770
					Efficiencies of low elasticity[a] specification				
Land	0.760	0.811	0.832	0.691	0.761	0.924[b]	0.811	0.882[b]	0.824[b]
Labor	0.906	0.972	0.930	0.960	0.936	0.934	0.949	0.971	0.963
Capital	0.869	0.836	0.583	0.832	0.807	0.558	0.745	0.824	0.743

a. The elasticities in question are elasticities of variable input demands with respect to fixed input.
b. The subsidized input demand (land if several inputs are subsidized) became perfectly inelastic at a price above the subsidized price.

subsidies varies markedly across industries (see the fourth and eighth columns of table 25). The minerals industry, for which land is least substitutable for other inputs (see table 25), has a very high efficiency with only a 5 percent deadweight loss. The paper industry, for which the estimated land-capital elasticity of substitution is very high, has a deadweight loss of nearly a third. Table 26 compares this land price subsidy with equally beneficial subsidies on labor or capital prices. The qualitative results here should come as no surprise since the comparisons are similar in principle to those done for the restricted loan guarantee. Two points are worth emphasizing, however.

First, altering the assumed responsiveness of variable input demands with respect to publicly provided inputs has little effect on the relative merits of alternative subsidies on *variable* inputs. Second, although labor price subsidies dominate both capital price and land price subsidies, land price subsidies do not appear nearly as attractive relative to capital subsidies as in the analysis of loan guarantees. The reason for this latter result is that in nearly all cases in table 26, in contrast to the loan guarantee simulations, the demand for land does not become perfectly inelastic within the subsidized price range, and thus the average efficiency of subsidies is not driven up in the manner described in the analysis of loan guarantees. (In table 26, too, however, the efficiency of land subsidies is generally high when the demand for land becomes perfectly price-inelastic, as is indicated by footnote b in the table). Only for the "other" industry group are land price subsidy efficiencies below 90 percent when the demand for land turns perfectly inelastic, and in this case it so happens that demand turns perfectly inelastic just barely above the subsidized price.[2]

Simulating Publicly Provided Inputs

The most difficult and tenuous comparison is that between the land price subsidy of table 25 and equally beneficial subsidies in the form of higher levels of publicly provided inputs. This comparison raises important problems of measurement.

Problems of Measurement

There are problems of measurement with regard to both the price and the quantity of publicly provided goods. Each will be discussed in turn.

Identifying the marginal social cost of variable inputs is a much less nettlesome problem than finding a comparable social cost for fixed inputs. The marketplace offers prices for variable inputs, and even in the face of monopolistic elements in the economy, these market prices are likely to give a reasonable range for marginal social costs—and will often provide very good estimates. (Even in the face of artificial government requirements, for example, the marginal social cost of credit to small and medium-sized firms usually lies between the bank and curb rates.) Firms do not purchase publicly provided inputs, however, and the marginal social cost of such fixed inputs is much more problematic since there is no market in which to observe how much firms are willing to pay for these factors.

The simulations that follow evaluate the marginal social costs of fixed factors in two ways. First, costs are evaluated at a preset number that is provided to the simulation model by the user. In ideal circumstances this number would be based on cost studies that indicate how much the government must pay to provide various levels of public services. But even in the present less than ideal circumstances, the use of a fixed base allows comparisons across industries and across firm sizes that a sliding scale of marginal costs could not easily accommodate.

Second, the costs are evaluated at their initial marginal shadow value to a firm. That is, the change in the firm's costs that would result from a one-unit increase in a publicly provided input is computed. This shadow value of the input is the amount the firm would be willing to pay for that fixed input. If publicly provided inputs had no public-goods aspects, this would be the appropriate marginal cost as long as publicly provided inputs were available initially in an optimizing mix. This idealistic scenario warrants the use of shadow values as an interesting basis for evaluating deadweight losses. There are, however, two limitations in using shadow values in this way. The first is the obvious point that publicly provided inputs are likely to have at least some public-goods aspects, and consequently the conditions for Pareto optimality require marginal costs to be set to something besides the input's shadow value for a single firm. The second is a more important point. Differences in the shadow values of publicly provided inputs across industries will yield incomparable deadweight loss estimates across industries if the deadweight losses are computed using the specific shadow prices of publicly provided inputs for each industry as the values of fixed inputs. This arises because in such cases the social prices for computing deadweight losses would be different for each industry or output level.

Publicly Provided Inputs versus Land Price Subsidies

Table 27 reports the efficiencies of land price subsidies (taken from table 25) under high and low elasticities of variable input demand with respect to fixed infrastructure. The table also reports the efficiencies of equally beneficial subsidies in the form of increased infrastructure. The second and fifth rows provide the efficiencies of the infrastructure subsidies premised on the marginal social cost being equal to the initial shadow value of the fixed infrastructure for a firm in the industry. Since the shadow values differ from industry to industry, these measures of efficiency do not permit cross-industry comparisons. The third and sixth rows provide the efficiencies of the infrastructure subsidies premised on a single, albeit arbitrary, social cost for fixed infrastructure. These measures permit cross-industry comparisons of relative efficiency but offer no insight into the actual levels of these efficiencies in any industry.

Despite the limitations of the measures of efficiency of infrastructure subsidies in table 27, some insights persist. In particular, the relative efficiency of subsidies in the form of higher fixed inputs depends crucially on the substitutability of the fixed inputs for variable inputs, as the theoretical discussion of chapter 1 leads one to expect. The efficiencies of fixed input subsidies drop markedly when the assumed elasticities of variable input demand fall in magnitude, no matter how fixed inputs are evaluated. Second, the second and fifth rows of table 27 show that unless the social cost of publicly provided inputs is well below the shadow value of those inputs to the firm, land subsidies sharply dominate increases in publicly provided goods for all industries. This conclusion can be strongly drawn if one judges the high elasticity specification to be an upper bound on the substitutability of publicly provided inputs for variable inputs.

Publicly Provided Goods and Firm Size

Just as nettlesome as the pricing of publicly provided inputs is their quantification. The difficulty here is not in measuring

Table 27. Efficiencies of Land Price and Fixed Input Quantity Subsidies Equal to 75 Percent Land Price Subsidy

Subsidy mechanism	Food	Textiles	Wood	Paper	Chemicals	Minerals	Basic metals	Fabricated metals	Other
				High elasticity[a] specification					
Land price	0.776	0.831	0.862	0.680	0.782	0.950	0.800	0.912	0.835
Fixed inputs (shadow value[b])	0.663	0.768	0.441	0.763	0.584	0.692	0.700	0.712	0.899
Fixed inputs (preset value[b])	0.789	0.904	0.301	1.008	0.430	1.147	1.636	0.621	2.166
				Low elasticity[a] specification					
Land price	0.760	0.811	0.832	0.691	0.761	0.924[c]	0.811	0.882[c]	0.824[c]
Fixed inputs (shadow value[b])	0.441	0.566	0.299	0.511	0.355	0.470	0.506	0.526	0.815
Fixed inputs (preset value[b])	0.291	0.335	0.098	0.404	0.152	0.435	0.390	0.274	1.020

a. Elasticities in question are elasticities of variable input demands with respect to fixed input.

b. See text.

c. The subsidized input demand (land if several inputs are subsidized) became perfectly inelastic at a price above the subsidized price.

government investments. Miles of road or megawatts of electricity transmission capacity—or even distance from the city center—are not unacceptable devices for measurement. But one must ask how firms of different sizes respond to government investment in a region. Most government investments offer benefits that can be realized anew with each increment to output, and consequently the input is in effect proportional to output. For example, every unit of output gets to the city center faster when the road system is improved. Conversely, some public investments are less exclusionary, and each firm gets access to them without regard to the level of output. For example, police surveillance deters breaking and entering for both small and large enterprises equally. In this view, publicly provided inputs are available in fixed quantities independent of a firm's level of output.

This section does not explore in detail the consequences of externality or the public-goods aspects of publicly provided inputs. But it does explore the two extremes: benefits from publicly provided inputs accruing in proportion to output and the effective levels of those inputs when independent of output.[3]

The cost model assumes that the technology is linearly homogeneous in *all* inputs; that is, doubling both variable and fixed inputs will double output (and costs). Consequently the percentage results in tables 25–27 pertain to *all* output levels for a firm if publicly provided inputs yield their benefits in proportion to output (that is, if the quantity of a publicly provided input at a given location is proportional to the firm's size). Although this view of publicly provided inputs is convincing, some independence of the effective quantity of public inputs from firms' output levels is likely. Consequently tables 28–30 recalculate the high elasticity specification results of tables 25–27 for large and small firms under the hypothesis that the effective levels of government inputs in an area are independent of the quantity produced. Such complete independence is an extreme that permits the results to be bounded. The truth of the matter, however, is likely to lie much closer to tables 25–27.

The simulations underlying the present analysis of firm size and public infrastructure subsidies assume that large firms have output and cost levels approximately equal to the means for firms in the industry that have outputs above the overall industry mean. The simulations also assume that small firms have output and cost levels equal to the means for firms in the

Table 28.   Benefits and Deadweight Loss
from 75 Percent Land Subsidy Given No Variation
of Fixed Input Effects with Output

	Low-output firms		High-output firms	
Industry	Benefits as a fraction of firm's cost	Benefits as a fraction of subsidy cost	Benefits as a fraction of firm's cost	Benefits as a fraction of subsidy cost
Food	0.084	0.983	0.222	0.702
Textiles	0.076	0.959	0.144	0.734
Wood	0.099	0.998	0.303	0.748
Paper	0.179	0.637	0.108	0.744
Chemicals	0.078	0.989	0.227	0.697
Minerals	0.079	1.000	0.299	0.802
Basic metals	0.139	0.906	0.215	0.742
Fabricated metals	0.042	1.000	0.176	0.716
Other	0.102	0.893	0.132	0.781

industry that have outputs below the overall mean for the
industry. Consequently each industry has different low and high
cost and output levels. This suggests caution in comparing
across industries within high and low output levels.

It is, however, useful to focus on comparisons across high and
low output levels within industries and to ask what results then
generalize across industries. To facilitate comparisons across
output levels, tables 28–30 assume that all firms pay the bank
rate of interest. To interpret this specification it is suitable to
say that the tables analyze the marginal effect of land price
subsidies for firms that have already been given loan guarantees
as long as the true social cost of credit is the bank rate—a quite
realistic view of the situation in, say, Banwoel.

In table 28, benefits from a land price subsidy rise as a fraction of firm costs as output rises, while the efficiency of the
subsidy falls as output rises. This result appears to reflect the
fact that land is a better substitute (according to table 14) for
the publicly provided inputs than are other inputs. Therefore
larger firms, being relatively more "starved" for publicly
provided inputs (the ratio of fixed inputs to output falls with
firm size under this specification's interpretation of publicly
provided inputs), make a larger substitution toward land when

Table 29. Efficiencies of Land, Labor, and Capital Price Subsidies Yielding Benefits Equal to 75 Percent Land Price Subsidy Given No Variation of Fixed Input Effects with Output

Price subsidized	Food	Textiles	Wood	Paper	Chemicals	Minerals	Basic metals	Fabricated metals	Other
					Low-output firms				
Land	0.983[a]	0.050	0.009[a]	0.637	0.989[a]	1.000[a]	0.906[a]	1.000[a]	0.893[a]
Labor	0.981	0.989	0.982	0.969	0.584	0.990	0.983	0.980	0.953
Capital	0.909	0.874	0.854	0.427	0.904	0.529	0.997	0.538	0.874
					High-output firms				
Land	0.702	0.734	0.748	0.744	0.697	0.802	0.742	0.916	0.781
Labor	0.816	0.958	0.864	0.958	0.882	0.835	0.859	0.930	0.970
Capital	0.861	0.819	0.488[a]	0.898	0.755	0.438	0.829	0.770	0.579

a. The subsidized input demand (land if several inputs are subsidized) became perfectly inelastic at a price above the subsidized price.

Table 30. Efficiencies of Land Price and Fixed Input Quantity Subsidies Equal to 75 Percent Land Subsidy Given No Variation of Fixed Input Effects with Output

Subsidy mechanism	Food	Textiles	Wood	Paper	Chemicals	Minerals	Basic metals	Fabricated metals	Other
					Low-output firms				
Land price	0.983[a]	0.959[a]	0.998[a]	0.637	0.989[a]	1.000[a]	0.906[a]	1.000[a]	0.893
Fixed inputs (shadow value)[b]	0.857	0.863	0.728	0.800	0.811	0.808	0.798	0.873	0.919
Fixed inputs (preset value)[b]	0.034	0.101	0.058	0.063	0.055	0.061	0.132[a]	0.035	0.039
					High-output firms				
Land price	0.702	0.734	0.748	0.744	0.697	0.802	0.742	0.716	0.781
Fixed inputs (shadow value)[b]	0.579	0.672	0.231	0.785	0.403	0.498	0.589	0.494	0.912
Fixed inputs (preset value)[b]	5.717	4.587	1.061	4.827	1.873	4.798	15.619	3.212	71.660

a. The subsidized input demand (land if several inputs are subsidized) became perfectly inelastic at a price above the subsidized price.
b. See text.

land's price falls than do smaller firms. This shift raises both benefits and deadweight loss, but raises the latter by more.

In table 29, the efficiencies of alternative subsidies on labor and capital fall as output rises. Large firms appear to have greater possibilities for substitution among variable inputs than do smaller firms, and consequently they show greater deadweight losses. This greater substitutability is also evident in table 30 when an increase in the quantity of the publicly provided input is examined. In the third and sixth rows the social cost of the fixed input is set equal to the marginal value of the fixed input for a typical-size firm rather than for a small or large firm. When the social costs of the fixed inputs are set equal to this arbitrary single price for both large and small firms, the larger firms always value the fixed input more highly and therefore suffer smaller deadweight losses. Indeed, the marginal value larger firms put on the fixed inputs is so large that deadweight losses would be *negative* (deadweight gains) if the marginal social cost were initially set to the marginal valuation typical-size firms place on the fixed input. This result suggests that large firms can be characterized as starved for the fixed input in these simulations.

Indeed, in general, if publicly provided inputs are independent of firms' output levels, individual firms will always disagree about the optimal level of public investment. Large firms will always want a higher level of public investment than small ones. If firms use publicly provided inputs in intensities proportional to output, however, disputes about public investment will tend to break along industry lines (as a result of differences in technologies) rather than by size of firm.

Notes

1. The price of land will vary with proximity to inputs and customers as well as with the extent of publicly provided infrastructure. Transport investments can influence this proximity, but land prices at remote sites will always be affected to some degree by their remoteness.

2. One might wonder if the difference in the efficiency of the land price subsidy depends critically upon the use of unrestricted cost functions in the analysis of loan guarantees and restricted cost functions here. Appendix C explores this issue and suggests that this is not the case.

3. In this section, I also abstract from the myriad complexities in how firms sometimes pay for publicly provided infrastructure. For example, I ignore that firms pay a marginal price for kilowatt hours but cannot purchase increased kilowatt capacity from the public sector; I also ignore that firms pay gasoline taxes which result in a feedback between investments and the marginal cost of transport—better roads increase road usage but lower the per mile use of gasoline.

CHAPTER 4

Conclusion

THE KOREAN GOVERNMENT'S economic policies use many devices to influence firms' location decisions. Mandates, prohibitions, tax breaks, loan guarantees, land price reductions, promises of public infrastructure investments, and wage bill subsidies are all used to alter the spatial outcomes of the marketplace. Firms that move within the Seoul region have reported, however, that the most important government programs for them are guaranteed loans, land price reductions, and the provision of public infrastructure. These programs deliberately distort firms' location decisions to accomplish such other goals of national policy as pollution reduction, income redistribution, and military security. But most of the government's policies also unintentionally distort firms' production decisions—how firms mix land, labor, and capital in the production process.

The lessons drawn here are applied most reliably to Korea, but they are probably applicable in other countries where industrial location is a hot topic. Most of the qualitative conclusions I draw are robust across industries; they are not sensitive to mild variations in technology. Because industrial technology is remarkably homogeneous in cities throughout the world, it is likely that the simulation results reported here would be applicable to most other countries.

A successful industrial location policy induces a firm that would have chosen location A to choose location B, which the government prefers. The policy must overcome any cost or profit advantage that site A enjoys. In choosing among alternative policies, the government should ask, "Which politically feasible policy most cheaply overcomes site A's advantage?" The cheapest policy will be the one that induces the smallest distortion in a firm's production decisions.

Three important economic principles offer qualitative guidance in assessing alternative location policies. First, if a policymaker is limited to subsidizing the price of a single input to induce the firm to choose B over A, then it will be least costly

77

to subsidize an input that is used extensively by the firm and is a poor substitute for other inputs. Second, if a policymaker is limited to increasing the provision of a single public input (for example, public transportation), then it will be least costly to increase the provision of an input that the firm would be willing to pay much for and that is a good substitute for other inputs. Third, if sites A and B differ in some one factor price, or in some one publicly provided input, it may be better to subsidize a different factor's price or augment the provision of a different public input rather than close the gap between the two sites.

These principles allow the economic parameters necessary for assessing alternative location policies to be identified: the share of costs borne by each factor (factor shares), the marginal value to the firm of publicly provided inputs (shadow prices), and the substitutability of each factor for others (elasticities of substitution). The translog restricted cost function (developed in chapter 2) can be used with Korean census data to estimate these three sets of parameters for the Korean setting. The parameters estimated in chapter 2 are encouraging in their general conformity to similar estimates developed in other analyses. One feature is disappointing, however: variables intended to reflect the provision of public inputs appeared to have no effect on firms' costs. Only when a proxy for the aggregate of publicly provided inputs is included in the model are cost effects uncovered.

Public infrastructure investments are important for industrial production. Cities with poor roads, limited telecommunications, and unreliable electricity and water supplies are less productive than their capital-rich competitors. But incorporating the productivity of public infrastructure into an econometric model of individual firms' costs raises problems of practical and theoretical measurement that have not been solved satisfactorily. Perhaps detailed case studies of the costs of specific firms and the uses to which they put public infrastructure would advance understanding of these issues.

Since guaranteed loans, land price reductions, and public infrastructure investments are the government programs firms cite as most important, chapter 3 dealt with simulations of them. Wage bill subsidies were also analyzed because the high factor share of labor suggests that they would be particularly efficient.

The evidence from the simulations indicates that the variations in efficiencies and subsidy benefits across industries are small relative to the variations across types of subsidies. Therefore these final paragraphs discuss the findings on the various subsidies. If, as seems likely, the inability of small and medium-sized firms to obtain bank loans is an artificial constraint resulting from government policies, the message from the simulations is clear. Loan guarantees are a highly cost-effective tool for location policy. Perhaps 20 percent of the subsidy payments granted to firms through loan guarantees will be recouped through the increased social efficiency of input choices by the firms that benefit.

Quite apart from industrial location policy itself, this observation raises important questions about the government policies that restrict the access of small and medium-sized firms to bank credit. These restrictions may result in efficiency losses equal to as much as 4 percent of the land, labor, and capital costs incurred by the manufacturing sector. Certainly one must question the wisdom of such policies.

Of course there may be good reasons for the government's credit policies. But given the magnitude of the costs, the reasons need careful thought. Are the objectives of the credit policies misserved by the loan guarantees used in industrial location policies? The simulations do not touch upon these interactions between location policies and other objectives of the Korean government, but such interactions must be considered by policymakers who wish to make good use of the findings reported here.

If the Korean government were to alter its policy of credit rationing, subsidies to the price of labor would become the most efficient devices for relocating firms. This finding is not particularly surprising on theoretical grounds—the cost share of labor is high, and that suggests relatively high efficiency. But there is some surprise since the Korean government has relied only little on subsidies of this form in its efforts to influence choices of location. Indeed, wage bill subsidies appear to be more efficient than the currently popular land price subsidies favored by the government.

Less clear from the simulations are the relative merits of subsidies to fixed and variable inputs. If the marginal social costs of private fixed inputs are anywhere near their shadow values to individual firms, subsidies to fixed inputs are dominated by subsidies to variable inputs. Most fixed inputs are public goods, however, or at least quasi-public goods.[1] Therefore the comparison of shadow value with shadow cost is not wholly appropriate for these inputs since the optimal choice of public goods depends on the sum of the shadow values across firms, not on the shadow value of one firm in isolation.

This last observation highlights one important feature of subsidies of public goods: the more densely populated the area in which the investments are made, the more efficient the subsidies. Since one aim of relocation policy is to deconcentrate economic activity, subsidies to fixed inputs are likely to be less efficient in areas where from a policy point of view they are most wanted by policymakers. This does not imply that fixed input subsidies cannot dominate variable input subsidies on the outskirts of the city. But for such dominance the marginal social cost of the fixed input must be lower than it would have to be in a more densely populated area.

Before a fuller evaluation of the efficiency of fixed input subsidies can be conducted, further research on the costs of such investments must be done. The simulations in the previous chapter were sharply constrained by the absence of such cost information.

A second issue related to subsidies on fixed inputs is the relation between firm size and publicly provided inputs. At one extreme, one could view publicly provided inputs as available to all firms in a single fixed quantity. At the other extreme, one could view these inputs as available in proportion to a firm's output.

The simulations reveal that a literal application of the former view leads to markedly more variation in total land, labor, and capital costs as output varies than is observed in the data from Korean manufacturing. Hence this study leans toward the latter view under which the relative attractiveness of fixed input subsidies is independent of the level of output.

Some publicly provided inputs are likely to fit the first mold better, however. To the extent that they do, the relative benefits and efficiency of fixed input subsidies will vary with firm size. The simulations indicate that in the face of literally constant fixed inputs, the balance of efficiency tilts toward fixed input subsidies and away from variable input subsidies as the level of output rises.

Finally, the simulations suggest that returns to scale may be of greater interest than was initially thought. Loan guarantees alter the marginal cost of output by a factor of about two. Such large alterations in a marginal cost could have considerable effect on the level of output selected by the firm even if the returns to scale are fairly close to unity (as the evidence suggests). This result is confirmed in casual surveys of Korean firms receiving such guarantees. It was not uncommon to find them doubling their output. The consequences of such effects on output level for the overall efficiency of industrial location policy (or credit allocation policies) should be taken into account. The focus of this study, however, has been on the relative efficiencies of mechanisms yielding equal benefits to the firm. Therefore it has been less concerned with the differentials across policies, and the differentials in output inefficiencies are likely to be small given the observed pattern of nearly constant marginal costs.

Note

1. Fixed inputs are often networks, such as roads, water and sewer lines, electricity grids, and telephone links. Whenever these are uncongested even part of the time, there will be a public or quasi-public good aspect to the input.

A Formal Analysis of Alternative Policies for Industrial Location

THIS APPENDIX DEVELOPS a formal analysis of the relative efficiencies of alternative relocation policies. The policies considered are all intended to induce a firm to choose one particular site rather than another. To be successful, each must offer the firm some level of benefits, $\bar{B}$, sufficient to make the government's preferred site as profitable as the firm's preferred location in the absence of the policy. By the relative efficiency of two policies is meant the difference in the net social worth of the bundles produced by the firm under the two policies, given that both are successful in yielding the firm benefits $\bar{B}$. The total inefficiency of policies would also include the social cost ($\bar{B}$ in the case of no externalities and optimal provision of public services) of not locating at the firm's most desirable location.

These analyses of the cost to the government of relocating the firm are richer than the usual economist's fare. All too frequently, economists point out that the cheapest way to achieve a policy goal such as relocation is to make a cash grant. Unfortunately such simplistic policies are often not feasible, whatever their economic virtues. In the following, I try to look realistically for optimal policies in the face of restrictions on feasible policies. Thus, for example, I establish conditions for determining mechanisms for price and quantity subsidies when firms are able to vary some inputs but must take others as fixed and when the government must choose its policies from a set of politically feasible subsidy schemes.

The first analyses are limited to location policies that rely on price mechanisms. These analyses will be familiar to many readers; they are very similar to the consumer analyses found in Diamond and McFadden (1974). The analysis of price mechanisms provides a comfortable path to the less familiar analysis of nonprice mechanisms that follows. Extending the analysis to embrace the nonprice mechanisms will simply require replacing the unrestricted cost and profit functions suitable for studying price mechanisms with their restricted counterparts. The analyses are conducted in the same spirit as the consumer behavior studies of Latham (1980) and Kennedy and MacMillan (1980).

To demonstrate the power of cost and profit functions for comparing policies, the following eight questions will be answered:

- If only one input price is to be subsidized, which input should be chosen if the firm must receive benefits $\bar{B}$ to be induced to choose this site?
- If several (but not necessarily all) inputs are to be subsidized, what are the optimality conditions for the subsidies?
- Would it be optimal to achieve the required benefits at this site by offering the firm the prices that prevail at the alternative site? In particular, if two sites differ only in the transportation costs of inputs, is it an optimal (second-best) solution to offer to pay differential transport costs? Or if two sites differ only with regard to one input price, should that input be subsidized rather than another?
- Are price subsidies more attractive to firms for which the deadweight loss from the subsidy would be larger?
- If only one input provided by the government rather than bought by the firm is to be increased, which input should be chosen if the firm must receive benefits $\bar{B}$?
- If several inputs provided by the government are to be increased, what are the conditions of optimality for these increases?
- What is the optimal mix of price and nonprice mechanisms for inducing a move, given that not all prices and inputs can be altered?
- When are nonprice mechanisms more efficient than price mechanisms?

The notation for the technical analysis is as follows. Let y be the output of the firm, q be a vector of privately purchased inputs, and s a vector of publicly provided inputs. Let p_y be the price of output, p be a vector of input prices for q, and r a vector of input prices for s. The firm's production function is $y = f(q,$

s), the cost function corresponding to f is $c = c(p, s, y)$, and the profit function corresponding to f is $\pi = \pi(p_y, p, s)$. A restricted profit function corresponding to a set of constraints of the form $q_i \leq \bar{q}_i$, $i = 1, \ldots, n$, is denoted by $\bar{\pi} = \bar{\pi}(p_y, p, s, \bar{q})$. To begin with, however, s and $\bar{q}$ will be ignored. Only purchased inputs, their prices, and output in the long run will be considered.

The subsidy paid by the government, S, is defined as the difference between the market value of the bundle of inputs chosen under the subsidy and the payments made by the firm for the inputs at subsidized prices. Market prices are denoted p_m and subsidized prices p.

$$(\text{A-1}) \qquad S = \sum_{i=1}^{n} (p_i^m - p_i) \frac{\delta C(p, y)}{\delta p_i}$$

(Recall that the derivative of the cost function is the conditional demand for the input.)

The benefits to the firm, B, are defined as the reduction in costs incurred as a result of the subsidy.

$$(\text{A-2}) \qquad B = C(p^m, y) - C(p, y)$$

$$= \sum_{i=1}^{n} p_i^m \frac{\delta C(p^m, y)}{\delta p_i} - \sum_{i=1}^{n} p_i \frac{\delta C(p, y)}{\delta p_i}$$

The economic loss associated with the subsidy is therefore:

$$(\text{A-3}) \quad L = S - B = \sum_{i=1}^{n} p_i^m \frac{\delta C(p, y)}{\delta p_i} - \sum_{i=1}^{n} p_i^m \frac{\delta C(p^m, y)}{\delta p_i} \geq 0$$

with the inequality following from the fact that $\delta C(p_m, y) / \delta p_i$, $i = 1, \ldots, n$, is the cost-minimizing vector of qs for $p = p_m$.

One Input Subsidized

The choice of which input to subsidize turns on two factors: the substitutability of one factor for another, and the amount of each factor in use. To see this, let us ask how inefficiency, L, varies with benefits, B, when benefits are transmitted by subsidizing one input, say q_i.

From equation A-2 we obtain by differentiation

$$1 = - \frac{\delta C(p, y)}{\delta p_i} \cdot \frac{dp_i}{dB}$$

$(C[p_m, y]$ is fixed as p_i changes.) Hence

$$\frac{dp_i}{dB} = - \frac{1}{\dfrac{\delta C(p, y)}{\delta p_i}} = - \frac{1}{q_i(p, y)}$$

Differentiating equation A-3, we obtain

$$(A\text{-}4) \qquad \frac{\delta L}{\delta B} = \sum_{j=1}^{n} p_j^m \frac{\delta^2 C(p, y)}{\delta p_i} \cdot \frac{dp_i}{dB} = - \frac{\displaystyle\sum_{j=1}^{n} p_j^m \frac{\delta q_j}{\delta p_i}}{q_i}$$

which indicates that choosing to subsidize a good used in large quantity ($q_i >> 0$) or a good which is not much of a substitute for others will reduce the inefficiency incurred in granting benefits. (The term $\sum_{j=1}^{n} p_j^m \delta q_j / \delta p_i$ is negative when $p_i < p\,_i^m$ because an increase in p_i would reduce spending on q_i by more than it would raise spending on the other inputs when value is evaluated at p^m. This is precisely why the firm would choose less q_i at p_i^m than at p_i.)

The following two concepts will appear frequently below. The expression α_i^{ms} is the budget share of the quantity of the ith input picked at subsidized prices when evaluated at market prices:

$$\alpha_i^{ms} = \frac{p_i^m q_i\,(p, y)}{\displaystyle\sum_{j=1}^{n} p_j^m q_j\,(p, y)}$$

The expression θ_i^{ms} is the elasticity of the cost of inputs chosen at subsidized prices evaluated at the market price:

$$\theta\,_i^{ms} = \frac{p_i^m}{\displaystyle\sum_{j=1}^{n} p_j^m q_j\,(p, y)} \cdot \frac{\delta[\Sigma\, p_j^m q^i\,(p, y)]}{\delta p_i}$$

$$= \frac{p_i^m q_i}{\displaystyle\sum_{j=1}^{n} p_j^m q_j} \cdot \frac{1}{q_i} \cdot \sum_{i=1}^{n} p_j^m \frac{\delta q_j}{\delta p_i}$$

Equation A-4 thus becomes

$$(A-4') \qquad \frac{\delta L}{\delta B} = -\frac{\theta_i^{ms}}{\alpha_i^{ms}}$$

The rule of thumb for subsidy schemes which equation A-4 suggests is to subsidize a good that makes up a relatively large part of the firm's outlays and that is not easily substituted for. Another way to view equation A-4 is that the denominator indicates that when α_i is large, only a small change in price is needed to confer a given level of benefits. The numerator indicates the extent to which any particular change in price distorts consumption.

Optimal Subsidy Schemes

Suppose the government will subsidize a given subset of inputs $q_i, \ldots, q_k, k \leq n$. What are the optimality conditions for the subsidy scheme given the requirement that firms receive benefits $\bar{B}$ from the subsidies?

We wish to minimize:

$$L = \sum_{i=1}^{n} P_i^m \frac{\delta C(p, y)}{\delta p_i} - \sum_{i=1}^{n} p_i^m \frac{\delta C(p^m, y)}{\delta p_i}$$

subject to $B = \bar{B}$. Form the Lagrangian

$$\zeta = \Sigma p_i^m q_i - \Sigma p_i^m q_i^m + \lambda [\bar{B} - C(p^m, y) + C(p, y)]$$

The first-order conditions are:

$$\frac{\delta \zeta}{\delta p_i} = \sum_{j=1}^{n} p_j^m \frac{\delta q_j}{\delta p_i} + \lambda \frac{\delta C(p, y)}{\delta p_i} = 0 \qquad i = 1, \ldots, k$$

or

$$-\frac{\sum_{j=1}^{n} p_j^m \frac{\delta q_j}{\partial p_i}}{q_i} = \lambda \qquad i = 1, \ldots, k$$

That is,

$$(A-5) \qquad \frac{\theta_i^{ms}}{\alpha_i^{ms}} = \frac{\theta_j^{ms}}{\alpha_j^{ms}} \qquad i, j = 1, \ldots, k$$

plus $B = \bar{B}$.

Condition A-5 can also be expressed in terms of the Allen

elasticities of substitution (AES). The AES between goods s and t, σ_{st}, can be expressed (Blackorby, Primont, and Russell 1978) as:

$$\sigma_{st} = \frac{C(p,\,y)\,\dfrac{\delta^2 C}{\delta p_s\,\delta p_t}}{q_s\,q_t}$$

thus

$$\frac{p_s^m\,q_s\,\sigma_{st}}{C(p,\,y)} = \frac{p_s^m\,\dfrac{\delta^2 C}{\delta p_s\,\delta p_t}}{q_t}$$

and

$$\frac{\displaystyle\sum_{s\,=\,1}^{n}\sigma_{st}\,p_s^m q_s}{C(p,\,y)} = \frac{\displaystyle\sum_{s\,=\,1}^{m} p_s^m\,\dfrac{\delta^2 C}{\delta p_s\,\delta p_t}}{q_t}$$

Consequently, condition A-5 can be expressed as

(A-5') $\displaystyle\sum_{\ell\,=\,1}^{n}\sigma\ell_i\,\alpha\ell^{ms} = \sum_{\ell\,=\,1}^{n}\sigma\ell_j\,\alpha\ell^{ms}$ $i, j = 1, \ldots, k$

The tie of this result to the previous is obvious. One should first subsidize the input of which $\theta_i^{ms}/\alpha_i^{ms}$ is a minimum, as in the case above. When $\theta_i^{ms}/\alpha_i^{ms}$ for that input exceeds that for a second input, that second input should then be subsidized. This practice should be continued until $B = \bar{B}$.

In the special case of $k = n$, when all inputs can be subsidized, if the quantities of goods chosen at subsidized prices are the same as at market prices (which of course is achieved by equiproportionate subsidies), then

$$\Sigma p_j^m\,\frac{\delta q_i(p,\,y)}{\delta p_i} = \Sigma p_j^m\,\frac{\delta q_j\,(p^m,\,y)}{\delta p_i} = 0$$

This follows from the facts that (1) the demand for inputs is homogeneous of degree zero in input prices so that $\delta q_i\,/\,\delta p_i = \delta q_j^m\,/\,\delta p_i^m$ if $q_i = q_i^m$ and $p_j\,/\,p_i = p_j^m\,/\,p_i^m$ for all j, and (2):

$$q_i^m = \frac{\delta C\,(p^m,\,y)}{\delta p_i} = \frac{\delta \Sigma p_j^m\,q_j^m}{\delta p_i} = q_i^m + \sum_{j\,=\,1}^{n} p_j^m\,\frac{\delta q_j^m}{\delta p_i}$$

Hence, in this special case the first-order condition is met with $\lambda = 0$.

Matching the Alternative Site

Suppose prices are p in the site most attractive to the firm. Prices in the site that the government wants selected are p^m. Clearly the government can make the firm indifferent between the two sites by charging prices p at the second site also. When is this desirable? And when it is not desirable, what changes should be made?

Suppose that at the second site prices have been set at p, and the government now contemplates altering p_1 and p_2, keeping $B = \bar{B}$ as required. Thus

$$\Delta B = 0 = \frac{\delta C}{\delta p_1} \cdot \Delta p_1 + \frac{\delta C}{\delta p_2} \Delta p_2$$

hence

$$\frac{\Delta p_2}{\Delta p_1} = - \frac{\dfrac{\delta C}{\delta p_1}}{\dfrac{\delta C}{\delta p_2}} = - \frac{q_1\,(p, y)}{q_2\,(p, y)}$$

The effect on inefficiency of these price changes is

$$\left(\frac{dL}{dp_i}\right)_B = \frac{\delta L}{\delta p_1} + \left(\frac{dp_2}{dp_1}\right)_B \cdot \frac{\delta L}{\delta p_2}$$

$$= \sum_{j=1}^{n} p_j^m \frac{\delta q_j}{\delta p_1} - \frac{q_1}{q_2} \sum_{j=1}^{n} p_j^m \frac{\delta q_j}{\delta p_2}$$

This can be reformulated as

$$\frac{1}{q_1}\left(\frac{dL}{dp_1}\right)_B = \left(\frac{p_1^m \Sigma p_j^m q_j}{p_1^m \Sigma p_j^m q_j}\right) \frac{\Sigma p_j^m \dfrac{\delta h_j}{\delta p_1}}{q_1}$$

$$- \left(\frac{p_2^m \Sigma_j p_j q_j^m}{p_2^m \Sigma p_j^m q_j}\right) \frac{\Sigma p_j^m \dfrac{\delta q_j}{\delta p_2}}{q_2}$$

(A-6)
$$= \frac{\theta_1^{ms}}{\alpha_1^{ms}} - \frac{\theta_2^{ms}}{\alpha_2^{ms}}$$

Thus if goods 1 and 2 meet the conditions of optimality, no

change in these two prices is called for. If the difference in equation A-6 is not zero, however, a more efficient device to entice the firm to come to the desired site is available. The prices at the alternative site should not be matched.

In general, if two sites differ only with regard to one input price, it is possible that the optimal subsidy scheme is to subsidize still another good. As a particular example, if two sites differ only in the cost of transporting inputs from their sources, in general it is inappropriate to induce a choice of locating at the more costly site by offering to pay the differentials in transport costs.

These remarks would be trivial if one were always allowing for a first-best solution, that is, equiproportionate price subsidies. But the force of these comments comes from their applicability even in second-best cases in which only one of several inputs will be subsidized.

The Kind of Firm Drawn to the Subsidy

The deadweight losses induced by a price subsidy scheme yielding fixed benefits are smallest for the firms that both use much of the subsidized good and find it difficult to substitute for the subsidized good. For what sort of firm will a particular price subsidy be most attractive? The subsidy will appeal more to firms that use much of the subsidized good, and to firms that can substitute more easily for that good.

To see this, simply note that

$$\frac{\delta B}{\delta p_i} = - q_i$$

but

$$\frac{\delta^2 B}{\delta p_i^2} = - \frac{\delta q_i}{\delta p_i}$$

Hence firms with high q_i benefit more for each dollar of subsidy, but the marginal gains rise faster for firms whose consumption of q_i is more responsive to price. Firms for whom there is a large inframarginal benefit will be more attracted to price subsidies, which is good from the perspective of efficiency. But firms ready to respond more to the subsidy at the margin will also be more attracted, which is bad for efficiency.

Allowing for Output Effects

Little is changed in the above results by allowing the firm to alter its output in response to changes in factor prices. Benefits are altered in that altered revenues may shift benefits to the firm, and changes in input use will arise from output changes as well as substitution effects. But if one reinterprets θ_i^{ms} as the elasticity (with respect to the price of goods) of the market value of inputs net of increased revenues and evaluated at initial market prices, then all the formulas above would be repeated in an analysis based on profit functions rather than cost functions (except that total inefficiency would have to include any discrepancy between output's price and consumer's marginal valuation of the output).

If all inputs were purchased at set prices with or without distortions, the above analysis would suffice. In reality, however, some inputs are available only in fixed quantities at any given moment. Moreover, some governments' relocation mechanisms share this character: the government provides the firm with a fixed quantity of some good at no cost or at less than market cost. If the fixed quantities of goods do not coincide with the cost-minimizing or profit-maximizing amounts, then actual costs or profits will diverge from those that would be calculated from unrestricted cost or profit functions. If the government is providing an input to the firm, the firm's choices may also be distorted, although underprovision by the government can sometimes be overcome by private purchases to supplement the government's provisions.

The apparatus of restricted cost functions will now be introduced to enable us to incorporate analyses of nonprice relocation mechanisms into the general framework. The adaptation of the foregoing results on price mechanisms to include quantity restrictions will be clear from the discussion. Similarly, the extension of these results to profit functions from cost functions is straightforward and does not require elaboration.

Two common location policies, prohibitions and mandates, are not treated in this section. These policies do not alter the relative input prices in the target site, nor do they require increases in the provision of publicly provided goods. Consequently they induce no misallocation of resources except for their possible effect on optimal location per se.

The primary purpose of the following analysis is to establish that adaptations of the notions of cost or profit functions will permit one to analyze nonprice relocation mechanisms as well as price mechanisms. The approach taken to the firm here is similar to that taken to the consumer by Latham (1980) and Kennedy and MacMillan (1980).

First consider a policy that provides a firm with a fixed amount of the nth input, $\bar{q}_n$, at cost $C_n < p_n\bar{q}_n$. If

$$\bar{q}_n < \frac{\delta C(p, y)}{\delta p_n}$$

then the firm will accept the offer and augment the quantity $\bar{q}_n$. If $\bar{q}_n$ exceeds the firm's planned use of q_n, then it will accept the offer if costs would be lower by using $\bar{q}_n$ at cost C_n than otherwise, that is, if

$$C(p, y, \bar{q}) \le C(p, y)$$

where $C(p, y, \bar{q})$ denotes the cheapest way to produce y given that prices are p and that one uses $\bar{q}$ obtained at cost C_n.

It is of interest to allow the government to jointly offer $\bar{q}_n$ and alter other input prices, in which case the benefits to the firm from a policy are

$$B = C(p^m, y) - C(p, y, \bar{q})$$

The subsidy to the firm from such a policy would be

$$S = \sum_{i=1}^{n} p_i^m q_i^s - C(p, y, \bar{q})$$

where $q_1^s, \ldots, q_{n-1}^s$ are the quantities the firm would choose if prices were $p_1, \ldots, p_{n-1}$ given y and $\bar{q}_n$.

Holding C_n fixed, $C(p, y, \bar{q}_n) \le C(p, y, \bar{q}_{n_2})$ if $\bar{q}_{n_1} > \bar{q}_{n_2}$.

Furthermore

$$v_n = -\frac{\delta C(p, y, \bar{q}_n)}{\delta \bar{q}_n} \le p_n$$

if $\bar{q}_n > \delta C(p, y) / \delta p_n$ since otherwise it would pay the firm to purchase $\bar{q}_n$ without constraint. Also

$$\frac{\delta^2 C(p, y, \bar{q}_n)}{\delta^2 \bar{q}_n} \le 0$$

as it becomes increasingly difficult to substitute $\bar{q}_n$ for other inputs as q_n rises.

A striking result is that the derivatives of the restricted cost function with respect to factor prices still yield input demands, although now they are restricted demands conditioned on $q_n = \overline{q}_n$. To see this, let q^* minimize the cost of producing y at $p = p^*$ given $q_n = \overline{q}_n$. Then

$$g(p) = C(p, y, \overline{q}_n) - \sum_{i=1}^{n-1} p_i q_i^* - C_n \leq 0$$

reaches a maximum at $p = p^*$, and that implies

$$\frac{\delta g(p)}{\delta p_i} = \frac{\delta C(p, y, \overline{q}_n)}{\delta p_i} - q_i^* = 0$$

so

$$q_i^s = q_i(p, y, \overline{q}_n) = \frac{\delta C(p, y, \overline{q}_n)}{\delta p_i}$$

(Let $q_n^s = \overline{q}_n$).

As with price mechanisms, nonprice mechanisms generally bring deadweight losses:

$$L = S - B = \sum_{i=1}^{n} p_i^m q_i^s - \sum_{i=1}^{n} p_i^m q_i^m \geq 0$$

Now we can ask as before how deadweight loss changes with benefits, but here the benefits are altered by increasing $\overline{q}_n$ (holding C_n fixed).

$$\frac{\delta B}{\delta B} = 1 = -\frac{\delta C(p, y, \overline{q}_n)}{\delta \overline{q}_n} \cdot \frac{\delta \overline{q}_n}{\delta B}$$

$$\frac{\delta \overline{q}_n}{\delta B} = \frac{-1}{\delta C(p, y, \overline{q}_n) / \delta \overline{q}_n} = \frac{1}{v_n}$$

(A-7)
$$\frac{dL}{dB} = \sum_{i=1}^{n} p_i^m \frac{\delta q_i^s}{\delta \overline{q}_n} \cdot \frac{\delta \overline{q}_n}{\delta B} = \frac{\sum_{i=1}^{n} p_i^m \frac{\delta q_i^s}{\delta \overline{q}_n}}{v_n}$$

The intuition of this result is straightforward. First, if the shadow price of $\overline{q}_n$, $\overline{v}_n$ is low, a larger increase in $\overline{q}_n$ is needed to achieve a given increase in benefits. Second, a given increase in $\overline{g}_n$ can substitute for other inputs.

This relationship reflects a much more general result, just as equation A-4 reflected more general conditions of optimality. Consider a set of relocation mechanisms that alters the prices of some inputs and provides amounts of others that exceed what the firm itself would choose. Let $p_1, \ldots, p_n$ denote the prices of goods $q_1, \ldots, q_k$ that the firm buys in the marketplace, perhaps at distorted prices. Let $q_{k+1}, \ldots, q_n$ denote a vector of goods provided by the government for a set cost C_n. We shall now ascertain a set of optimality conditions for these mechanisms given benefits must equal some set level B. The problem, then, is to minimize

$$L = \sum_{i=1}^{n} p_i^m q_i^s - \sum_{i=1}^{n} p_i^m q_i^m$$

where $q_1^s, \ldots, q_n^s$ are the cost-minimizing input choices given $p_1, \ldots, p_k, y$, and $\bar{q}_{k+1}, \ldots, \bar{q}_n$. Also $q_j^s = \bar{q}_j, j = k+1, \ldots, n$. The constraint is that

$$\bar{B} = C(p^m, y^m) - C(p_1, \ldots, p_k, y, \bar{q}_{k+1}, \ldots, \bar{q}_n)$$
$$= C(p^m, y^m) - C^s$$

Form the Lagrangian

$$\zeta = L + \lambda(\bar{B} - B)$$

which yields the following first-order conditions

(A-8) $$\sum_{j=1}^{k} p_j^m \frac{\delta q_j^s}{\delta p_i} + \lambda \frac{\delta C^s}{\delta p_i} = 0 \qquad\qquad i = 1, \ldots, k$$

(A-9) $$\sum_{j=1}^{k} p_j^m \frac{\delta q_j^s}{\delta \bar{q}_i} + p_i + \lambda \frac{\delta C^s}{\delta \bar{q}_i} = 0 \qquad\qquad i = k+1, \ldots, n$$

$$\bar{B} = B$$

Conditions A-8 are simply the conditions of optimality for price mechanisms obtained above with restricted input demands replacing unrestricted input demands. Conditions A-9 indicate that dL/dB (see equation A-7) must be the same for each quantity $\bar{q}_{k+1}, \ldots, \bar{q}_n$, and must equal dL/dB for each price as well.

Reflection upon the conditions of optimality for price mechanisms in relation to those for nonprice mechanisms exposes a striking difference. Equation A-4 indicates that if p_i is manipulated,

$$\frac{dL}{dB} = -\frac{\Sigma p_j^m \dfrac{\delta q_j}{\delta p_i}}{q_i}$$

whereas equation A-7 says that if q_i is manipulated,

$$\frac{dL}{dB} = \frac{\sum\limits_{j=1}^{k} p_j^m \frac{\delta q_j}{\delta \overline{q}_i} + p_i}{v_i}$$

From an initial market solution, it will be more efficient to apply a nonprice subsidy to a good when that good has a high shadow price and is easily substituted for other goods. Price mechanisms will be more efficient when the good is used in large quantity and the good is not easily substituted for others.

The conditions of optimality for nonprice mechanisms have implications for nonprice relocation mechanisms that are analogous to those drawn earlier for price mechanisms. They firmly establish the power of the restricted cost function (and with simple adaptation, the restricted profit function) for analyzing how relocation policies alter firms' allocative efficiency.

Parameterizing the Translog Restricted Cost Function with User-Provided Elasticities and Factor Shares

THIS APPENDIX DISCUSSES how the simulation model converts user supplied data on elasticities of substitution, demand elasticities of variable inputs with respect to fixed inputs, and factor shares into parameters for the translog restricted cost function. The first step is to declare the initial conditions for the model. These include the levels of output and fixed inputs, the variable factor prices, and the level of total cost for which the user-provided elasticities and factor shares are presumed to hold.

There are two important cases to be considered. In the first, the technological data from other sources are assumed to be estimated under the same restrictions that apply to the translog restricted cost function. For example, if only publicly provided inputs are being held fixed, it seems reasonable to assume that these conditions correspond to the conditions under which most elasticities of substitution among capital and labor have been estimated (that is, with fixed levels of publicly provided inputs).

The second case is that in which the simulation model is holding fixed a quantity that was allowed to vary in the empirical studies. For example, to simulate a fixed-quantity capital subsidy, how can we adapt to our needs the estimates of the elasticity of substitution from studies in which capital was varying freely?

In the first case, if the available estimates of the elasticity of substitution are conditional on fixed levels of some inputs, such as publicly provided inputs, then the formula given above for the elasticity of substitution in terms of the cost function still applies. But the appropriate cost function is the restricted cost function:

$$\sigma_{ij} = \frac{v \dfrac{\delta^2}{\delta p_i \, \delta p_j}}{q_i q_j} \qquad\qquad i, j = 1, \ldots, k$$

$$i \neq j$$

Equation 2 above (see chapter 2) can be rewritten as

$$\frac{\delta v}{\delta p_i} = \frac{v}{p_i} \left(a_i + \sum_{j=1}^{k} \alpha_{ij} \ln p_j + \sum_{j=k+1}^{n} \gamma_{ij} \ln q_j + \tau_i \ln y \right) = \frac{v}{p_i} (S_i)$$

Thus it follows that

$$\frac{\delta 2_v}{\delta p_i \, \delta p_j} = \frac{v}{p_i p_j} \alpha_{ij} + \frac{S_i}{p_i} \frac{v}{p_j} \cdot S_j$$

Consequently, for the translog restricted cost function,

$$\sigma_{ij} = \frac{\alpha_{ij}}{S_i S_j} + 1$$

or

$$\alpha_{ij} = (\sigma_{ij} - 1) S_i S_j \qquad\qquad i, j = 1, \ldots, k$$

$$i \neq j$$

Thus the elasticities of substitution, coupled with equation 8 in chapter 2, allow us to fix all the γ_{ij}s once initial variable factor shares are specified.

Values for γ_{ij} are determined through knowledge of the elasticities of demand for the variable inputs with respect to the fixed inputs.

$$q_i = \frac{\delta v}{\delta p_i} = \frac{v}{p_i} (S_i) \qquad\qquad i = 1, \ldots, k$$

Therefore

$$\frac{\delta q_i}{\delta q_j} = \frac{v}{p_i q_j} \gamma_{ij} - \frac{S_i}{p_i} \cdot \frac{v}{q_j} S_j^* \qquad\qquad i = 1, \ldots, k$$

$$j = k + 1, \ldots, n$$

or

$$\epsilon_{ij} = \frac{q_j}{q_i} \frac{\delta q_i}{\delta q_j} = \frac{\gamma_{ij}}{S_i} - S_j^*$$

so that

$$\gamma_{ij} = (\epsilon_{ij} + S_j^*)\, S_i$$

The elasticities ϵ_{ij} used in the simulations reported in chapter 3 are drawn from the econometric work reported in chapter 2, and the initial shares of the variable inputs S_i used are those observed in Korea. The computer program will accept any ϵ_{ij} and S_i provided by the user. The shadow shares of the fixed inputs pose a more subtle problem because only the initial quantities of the fixed inputs are observed; we are in the dark about their shadow prices. Fortunately, we can indirectly retrieve the shadow shares of the fixed inputs from other variables.

The shadow value of the jth fixed input is simply the savings in other inputs that access to one more unit of that fixed input would yield. That is,

$$w_j = - \sum_{j=1}^{k} \frac{\delta q_i}{\delta q_j} \cdot p_j \qquad j = k+1, \ldots, n$$

so that

$$w_j\, q_j = - \sum_{k=1}^{k} \frac{q_i\, q_j}{q_i} \cdot \frac{\delta q_i}{\delta q_j}\, p_i$$

or

$$w_j\, q_j = - \sum_{i=1}^{k} p_i q_i\, \epsilon_{ij}$$

so that

$$S_j^* = \frac{w_j q_j}{v} = - \sum_{j=1}^{k} S_i\, \epsilon_{ij} \qquad j = k+1, \ldots, n$$

Hence γ_{ij} can be fixed by computing

$$\gamma_{ij} = (\epsilon_{ij} - \sum_{\ell=1}^{k} S_{\ell\epsilon}\, \epsilon_j)\, S_i \qquad \begin{array}{l} i = 1, \ldots, n \\ j = k+1, \ldots, n \end{array}$$

These numbers, coupled with equation A-7, then provide values for the τ_i as well.

With τ_i, v_{ij}, and α_{ij} all in hand, initial variable prices and shares for the variable inputs, initial fixed input quantities, and the initial output level permit us to calculate the a_i using equation 2. The only remaining parameters in the model are h_i, B_{ij}, and θ_i. Once B_{ij} is determined, equation 9 dictates the θ_i.

With θ_i and B_{ij}, the formula above for the S_i^*, coupled with equation 3, yields values for h_i.

Because of the limited information available regarding fixed inputs, the values of B_{ij} in the simulation model had to be set arbitrarily. Values were assumed to be consistent with the following conjectures: had firms been allowed to vary the fixed inputs at a marginal price equal to the shadow price, then the own-price elasticities of demand for the fixed inputs would be unitary and the cross-price elasticities among the fixed inputs would be zero.

The first conjecture has little effect on the present analyses since cross-price elasticities are much more important in determining deadweight loss and benefits than are own-price elasticities. The second conjecture has little effect because two fixed inputs are seldom considered in the analyses (so there is usually no cross-price effect needed in the models) and also because deadweight losses are driven more by cross effects between fixed and variable inputs or among variable inputs than between fixed inputs.

The link between B_{ij} and the as-if demand elasticities will be clearer as parameterization of the translog restricted cost function in the second case is now developed (which includes consideration of fixing an input that is variable in the available econometric studies).

For analytical tractability in this second case, we abstract from other fixed inputs. We thus find ourselves considering the relation between an unrestricted cost function and its restricted counterpart in which one input is fixed. The available econometric evidence pertains to an unrestricted cost function

$$C = c\,(p_1, \ldots, p_k, y)$$

The kth input is assumed to be fixed and $p = (p_1, \ldots, p_{k-1})$ is as needed. Since the available information on the elasticity of substitution and factor shares pertains to this unrestricted cost function and its derivatives, it is useful to explore the link between this set of equations and the restricted cost function $v\,(p, q_k, y)$ and its derivatives. The link is forged by noting that if p_k were equal to the shadow price of q_k at the fixed level in question (w_k), the firm (if left unrestricted) would choose to purchase just the restricted quantity q_k.

Consequently we find

$$H = c\,(p, w_k, y) = v\,(p, q_k, y) + w_k\,q_k$$

where the last term on the right reflects the fact that the restricted cost function yields only variable costs. The point is that for given p, if $p_k = w_k$, it does not matter whether the firm is restricted or not, because factor choices would be the same in either event.

It is very useful to explore some of the derivatives of H. (Throughout, $w_k = -\,\partial\gamma/\delta q^k$.)

$$\frac{\delta H}{\delta q_K} = \frac{\delta c\,(p, w_K, y)}{\delta q_K} = -\,\frac{\delta c}{\delta p_K}\cdot\frac{\delta^2 v}{\delta q_k^2}$$

and

$$\frac{\delta H}{\delta q_K} = \frac{\delta\,[v\,(p, q_K, y) + w_K\,q_K\,]}{\delta q_K} = -\,\frac{\delta^2 v}{\delta q_K}\cdot q_K$$

which confirms that

$$\frac{\delta c}{\delta p_K} = q_K$$

Similarly

$$\frac{\delta^2 H}{\delta q_K^2} = \frac{\delta^2 c}{\delta p_k^2}\left[\frac{\delta^2 v}{\delta q_K^2}\right]^2 - \frac{\delta c}{\delta p_K}\cdot\frac{\delta^3 v}{\delta q_K^3} = \frac{\delta^2 c}{\delta p_K^2}\left(\frac{\delta^2 v}{\delta q_K^2}\right) - q_K\,\frac{\delta^3 v}{\delta q_K^3}$$

and

$$\frac{\delta^2 H}{\delta q_K^2} = -\,\frac{\delta^3 v}{\delta q_K^3}\cdot q_K - \frac{\delta^2 v}{\delta q_K^2}$$

Thus

(B-1)
$$\frac{\delta^2 c}{\delta p_K^2} = \frac{-1}{\dfrac{\delta^2 v}{\delta q_K^2}}$$

when the left-hand side is evaluated at (p, w_k, y). Stated alternatively,

$$\frac{\delta q_K}{\delta p_K} = \frac{1}{\dfrac{\delta w_K}{\delta q_K}}$$

when the left-hand side is evaluated at (p, w_k, y), a result that should come as no surprise.

Next consider

$$\frac{\delta H}{\delta p_i} = \frac{\delta c}{\delta p_i} - \frac{\delta c}{\delta p_k} \cdot \frac{\delta^2 v}{\delta q_K \, \delta p_i}$$

so that

$$\frac{\delta^2 H}{\delta p_i \, \delta q_K} = -\frac{\delta^2 c}{\delta p_i \, \delta p_K} \cdot \frac{\delta^2 v}{\delta q_K{}^2} - \frac{\delta c}{\delta p_K} \cdot \frac{\delta^3 v}{\delta q_K{}^2 \, \delta p_i} + \frac{\delta^2 c}{\delta p_K{}^2}$$

$$\cdot \frac{\delta^2 v}{\delta q_K{}^2} \frac{\delta^2 v}{\delta q^2{}_K \, \delta p_i}$$

But by equation B-1,

$$\frac{\delta^2 c}{\delta p_K{}^2} \cdot \frac{\delta v}{\delta q_K{}^2} = -1$$

so

$$\frac{\delta^2 H}{\delta p_i \, \delta q_K} = -\frac{\partial^2 c}{\delta p_i \, \delta p_K} \cdot \frac{\delta^2 v}{\delta q_K{}^2} - \frac{\delta c}{\delta p_K} \cdot \frac{\delta^3 v}{\delta q_K{}^2 \, \delta p_i} - \frac{\delta^2 v}{\delta q_K \, \delta p_i}$$

But using the alternative form of H, we obtain

$$\frac{\delta^2 H}{\delta p_i \, \delta q_K} = -\frac{\delta^3 v}{\delta q_K{}^2 \, \delta p_i} \cdot q_K$$

Hence

(B-2)
$$\frac{\delta^2 c}{\delta p_i \, \delta p_K} = -\frac{\dfrac{\delta^2 v}{\delta q_K \, \delta p_i}}{\dfrac{\delta^2 v}{\delta q_K{}^2}}$$

Next consider

(B-3)
$$\frac{\delta H}{\delta p_i} = \frac{\delta c}{\delta p_i} - \frac{\delta c}{\delta p_K} \cdot \frac{\delta^2 v}{\delta q_K \, \delta p_i}$$

so that

$$\frac{\delta^2 H}{\delta p_i{}^2} = \frac{\delta^2 c}{\delta p_i{}^2} - \frac{\delta^2 c}{\delta p_i \, \delta p_K} \cdot \frac{\delta^2 v}{\delta q_K \, \delta p_i}$$

$$- \left[\frac{\delta^2 c}{\delta \, p_K \, \delta p_i} - \frac{\delta^2 c}{\delta p_K{}^2} \cdot \frac{\delta^2 v}{\delta q_K \, \delta p_i} \right] \frac{\delta^2 v}{\delta q_K \, \delta p_i}$$

$$- \frac{\delta c}{\delta p_K} \cdot \frac{\delta^3 v}{\delta q_K \, \delta p_i{}^2}$$

$$= \frac{\delta^2 c}{\delta p_i^2} - 2 \frac{\delta^2 c}{\delta p_i \, \delta p_K} \cdot \frac{\delta^2 v}{\delta q_K \, \delta p_i} + \frac{\delta^2 c}{\delta p_K^2} \left(\frac{\delta^2 v}{\delta q_K \, \delta p_i} \right)^2$$

$$- q_K \frac{\delta^3 v}{\delta q_K \, \delta p_i^2}$$

Using equations B-1 and B-2, we obtain

$$\frac{\delta^2 H}{\delta p_i^2} = \frac{\delta^2 c}{\delta p_i^2} + \frac{2 \left(\dfrac{\delta^2 v}{\delta q_K \, \delta p_i} \right)^2}{\dfrac{\delta^2 v}{\delta p_K^2}} - \frac{\left(\dfrac{\delta^2 v}{\delta p_K \, \delta p_i} \right)^2}{\dfrac{\delta^2 v}{\delta p_K^2}} - q_K \frac{\delta^3 v}{\delta q_K \, \delta p_i^2}$$

$$= \frac{\delta^2 c}{\delta p_i^2} + \frac{\left(\dfrac{\delta^2 v}{\delta q_K \, \delta p_i} \right)^2}{\dfrac{\delta^2 v}{\delta q_K^2}} - q_K \frac{\delta^3 v}{\delta q_K \, \delta p_i^2}$$

But once again, the alternative form of H yields another version:

$$\frac{\delta^2 H}{\delta p_i^2} = \frac{\delta^2 v}{\delta p_i^2} - \frac{\delta^3 v}{\delta p_i^2 \, \delta q_K} q_K$$

so

(B-4) $$\frac{\delta^2 c}{\delta p_i^2} = \frac{\delta^3 v}{\delta p_i^2} - \frac{\left(\dfrac{\delta^2 v}{\delta q_K \, \delta p_i} \right)^2}{\dfrac{\delta^2 v}{\delta q_K^2}}$$

Returning to equation B-3 and obtaining cross partials, we find:

$$\frac{\delta^2 H}{\delta p_i \, \delta p_j} = \frac{\delta^2 c}{\delta p_i \, \delta p_j} - \frac{\delta^2 c}{\delta p_i \, \delta p_K} \cdot \frac{\delta^2 v}{\delta q_K \, \delta p_j}$$

$$- \left[\frac{\delta^2 c}{\delta p_K \, \delta p_j} - \frac{\delta^2 c}{\delta p_K^2} \cdot \frac{\delta^2 v}{\delta q_K \, \delta p_j} \right] \frac{\delta^2 v}{\delta q_K \, \delta p_i}$$

$$- \frac{\delta^2 c}{\delta p_K} \cdot \frac{\delta^3 v}{\delta q_K \, \delta p_i \, \delta p_j}$$

$$= \frac{\delta^2 c}{\delta p_i \, \delta p_j} + \frac{\dfrac{\delta^2 v}{\delta q_K \, \delta p_i}}{\dfrac{\delta^2 v}{\delta p_K^2}} \cdot \frac{\delta^2 v}{\delta q_K \, \delta p_j} + \frac{\dfrac{\delta^2 v}{\delta q_K \, \delta p_j}}{\dfrac{\delta^2 v}{\delta q_K^2}} \cdot \frac{\delta^2 v}{\delta q_K \, \delta p_i}$$

$$-\frac{\dfrac{\delta^2 v}{\delta q_K\, \delta p_j}\cdot \dfrac{\delta^2 v}{\delta q_K\, \delta p_i}}{\dfrac{\delta^2 v}{\delta p_K{}^2}} - q_K\frac{\delta^3 v}{\delta q_K\, \delta p_i\, \delta p_j}$$

$$=\frac{\delta^2 c}{\delta p_i\, \delta p_j} + \frac{\dfrac{\delta^2 v}{\delta q_K\, \delta p_i}\cdot \dfrac{\delta^2 v}{\delta q_K\, \delta p_j}}{\dfrac{\delta^2 v}{\delta q_K{}^2}} - q_K\frac{\delta^3 v}{\delta q_K\, \delta p_i\, \delta p_j}$$

But the alternative form of H yields

$$\frac{\delta^2 H}{\delta p_i\, \delta p_j} = \frac{\delta^2 v}{\delta p_i\, \delta p_j} - \frac{\delta^3 v}{\delta q_K\, \delta p_i\, \delta p_j}\, q_K$$

So we find

(B-5)
$$\frac{\delta^2 c}{\delta p_i\, \delta p_j} = \frac{\delta^2 v}{\delta p_i\, \delta p_j} - \frac{\dfrac{\delta^2 v}{\delta q_K\, \delta p_i}\,\dfrac{\delta^2 v}{\delta q_K\, \delta p_i}}{\dfrac{\delta^2 v}{\delta q_K{}^2}}$$

Taken together, equations B-1, B-2, B-4, and B-5 permit strikingly simple characterizations of the links between the unrestricted and restricted cost functions. We obtain

(B-6a)
$$\frac{\delta^2 c}{\delta p_i\, \delta p_K} = \frac{\delta^2 v}{\delta q_K\, \delta p_i}\cdot \frac{\delta^2 c}{\delta p_K{}^2}$$

or

(B-6b)
$$\frac{\epsilon^u{}_{iK}}{\epsilon^u{}_{KK}} = \epsilon^r{}_{iK} \qquad i = 1,\ldots,K-1$$

where the terms on the left side are unrestricted price elasticities with respect to p_k, evaluated at (p, w_k, y) and the right side is the restricted demand elasticity for q_i with respect to q_k. And for elasticities of substitution in the restricted technology, $\sigma^r{}_{ij}$, we obtain:

(B-7)
$$(1+S^*{}_K)\sigma^r{}_{ij} = \sigma^u{}_{ij} - \frac{\sigma^u{}_{iK}\sigma^u{}_{jK}}{\sigma^u{}_{KK}} \qquad i,j=1,\ldots,K-1$$
$$i \neq j$$

where $\sigma^r{}_{ij}$ are the unrestricted elasticities of substitution.

And for the effect of q_k on w_k, we obtain:

(B-8)
$$\epsilon^{r}_{KK} = -\frac{1}{\epsilon^{u}_{KK}}$$

where the term on the left is the elasticity of the shadow price with respect to q_k and the term on the right is the unrestricted own-price elasticity for q_k.

One might guess that since the own- and cross-unrestricted demand elasticities are related by

(B-9)
$$\sum_{i=1}^{k} \rho_i \, \epsilon^{u}_{ik} = 0$$

where ρ_i is the unrestricted share of the ith input, and the value of ϵ^{r}_{KK} is determined through equations B-6b and B-8 once the ϵ^{r}_{iK} are set. This proves, however, not to be the case. What equation B-9 does imply is the finding above that the shadow share of q_k can be expressed in terms of the ϵ^{r}_{iK} and the shares of the variable inputs.

Application of equation B-8 to the specific case of the translog restricted cost function yields

$$B_{KK} = \frac{-S_K}{\epsilon_{KK}} - (1 + S_k) S_k$$

Thus the assumption of a unitary own-price elasticity of unrestricted demand at the shadow price yields

$$B_{KK} = -S_K^2$$

which is what is used here in the simulations for all publicly provided fixed inputs since there is no alternative information. More generally, equations B-6–B-8 have permitted unrestricted elasticities of substitution or demand to be translated into appropriate restricted elasticities that permit a restricted translog cost function to be parameterized using the transformed elasticities in the manner described earlier in this section.

One important activity carried out by the simulation model is to render convex the technology underlying the translog cost function. An unfortunate shortcoming of the translog specification is that for goods that have an elasticity of substitution less than one, the isoquants implied by the cost structure have concave segments. These segments are inconsistent with interior solutions to the cost minimization problem. Rather than cast aside the very useful translog function altogether, the simulation model adapts the model by, in effect, forcing the isoquants to become vertical or horizontal and remain so rather than become concave. This convexification of the isoquants underlying the cost function simply reflects an intuitively appealing idea: in the real world, the substitution relation that is most likely to give rise to negative elasticities of substitution (when the technology is approximated with a translog cost function) is indeed a zero elasticity of substitution.

Supplementary Simulation Results

THIS APPENDIX PRESENTS simulation results to supplement those reported in the text. The first set focused on land prices and firms' costs in an effort to lend credence to our use of distance from the center of the city as a measure of publicly provided inputs. The second set of simulations explored the relationship between restricted and unrestricted translog cost function specifications.

Simulations and Spatial Structure

The first simulation results reported in this appendix pertain to the spatial structure of the Seoul region. The inverse of the firm's distance from the city center is used as a measure of fixed nonpurchased inputs available to the firm. The mean distance in the sample is about 3 kilometers, so 0.333 is used as the base value of fixed inputs in specifying the simulation model.

When nonpurchased inputs are raised to 2.0 (0.5 kilometer from the city center), costs generally decline from 15 to 25 percent with a mean of about 25 percent. When these inputs are cut to 0.125 (8 kilometers from the city center), costs generally rise from 10 to 20 percent. The "other" industry category is the one outlier in these findings. This probably is caused by the relatively high demand elasticities for land and labor obtained for this category; see table 9 above. (This result is probably specious and arises from misspecifications in lumping all "other" manufacturing industries in one category.)

Table C-1 reports the mean change in costs from a base cost of about 115 as fixed inputs vary between 2.0 and 0.125. Below these changes are reported the net changes in costs that would occur if the altered levels of fixed inputs (distances) were accompanied by changes in land prices comparable to those observed at those distances in the Seoul region. As can be seen from the

Table C-1. Average Firm Costs for Alternative Fixed Input
Levels with and without Accompanying Land Price Changes

	Fixed input level				
Cost	2.0	1.0	0.333	0.20	0.125
With land price change fixed at 0.222	146	136	115	105	102
With land price changing[a]	119 (1.85)	124 (0.555)	115 (0.222)	116 (0.111)	112 (0.037)

a. The figure in parentheses is the assumed price of land.

table, the land price gradient very nearly neutralizes the fixed
input advantages or disadvantages of alternative locations.

This relatively good conformity of the simulation results
(except for the outlier "other" industries) indicates that the
parameterization of the industries is reasonably good, at least
for the typical-size firms for which these results are derived.
(The problems associated with firms of other sizes are discussed
below.) The good fit of the simulations does raise some concern,
however, about the appropriateness of using elasticities with
respect to distance as a proxy for elasticities with respect to
publicly provided inputs, even if the two are highly correlated.

Greater distance from the city center does not bring just lower
publicly provided inputs. Other problems also arise, most
particularly increased transportation costs. Consequently elasticities with respect to distance are probably an upper bound
on the magnitude of the elasticities with respect to publicly
provided inputs. In the above application, the relation between
the price gradient and the total effects of altered distance is of
interest, so there is no difficulty. But in the analyses in chapter
3, the interpretation desired is that of a publicly provided
input's effects on costs. Consequently in that chapter simulations are examined using reduced magnitudes for the elasticities
of variable inputs with respect to the fixed input.

Simulations and Duality

The last simulation reported demonstrates the dual nature of
price and quantity subsidies and supports the flipping back and

forth between restricted and unrestricted specifications in implementing the simulation model. For each quantity of subsidy the government can make, there is a corresponding price subsidy that yields the firm the same benefits and generates the same deadweight loss. This example focuses on only one industry—the food group. Table C-2 shows the specifications of elasticities for both an unrestricted and a restricted cost function for a firm receiving either price or quantity subsidies for capital when land and labor are the other two inputs.

Given prices for land and labor that reflect those paid by a typical firm and the choice of a firm with combined land and labor costs of 100 million won, initial capital holdings will be 6.7 units with a shadow value of 9.5 million won per unit. This is, roughly, the cost of capital for a typical firm that is paying the bank rate for credit.

When the restricted technology is used, offering the firm 1.1 additional units of capital reduces labor and land costs by 10 million won as the firm contracts its usage of those factors. The subsidized shadow price for land concomitantly drops to 7.98 million won per unit.

When the unrestricted specification of the technology is used, a subsidized price for capital of 7.98 million won per unit yields the firm 10.56 million won on 163 million won of total land, labor, and capital costs. Of these benefits, 0.13 million won result from lower capital costs and 10.43 million won from lower land and labor costs.

The difference between the 10 million and 10.43 million won

Table C-2. Restricted and Unrestricted Elasticities of Substitution for the Food Industry

Land-labor	Land-capital	Capital-labor
	Unrestricted	
0.25	0.75	0.85
(0.15)	(0.45)	(0.40)
	Restricted	
0.75	0.23	0.77[a]
(0.25)	(0.75)	(0.67)

Note: Shares in parentheses.
a. Elasticity of variable input demand.

benefits in the two simulations arises from two sources. First, the computations of elasticities were rounded, so the restricted and unrestricted elasticities do not correspond exactly. Second, the translog functional forms for the unrestricted and restricted cost functions are not duals to one another. Consequently the cost structures will not in general coincide over any finite range, even if their implicit elasticities match up properly at some point, as here. In this case, however, a discrepancy of 4 percent between the specifications suggests that moving back and forth between the restricted and unrestricted forms is tolerable as long as one makes the adjustments to elasticities described in the theoretical section above.

Fortran Simulation Code and Program Documentation

THE FORTRAN SIMULATION PROGRAM developed for this research is in no way specific to Korean policy. The user is free to specify any translog cost function and any combination of price and quantity subsidies. The program can be used in either interactive or batch mode. But the program was designed especially for interactive use, and the batch input mode requires input records that correspond to what would be called for by the program in the interactive mode. The inputs will depend on which options offered by the program the user wishes to use.

The program begins by prompting the user for the number of variable inputs and the number of fixed inputs. The maximum permitted for the former is 5; for the latter, 2. These numbers are entered as zero followed by the number of variable inputs, immediately followed by zero and the number of fixed inputs.

The second prompt asks the user to input the initial quantity of output and reminds the user that *unless otherwise directed* the user is to input all information with a decimal point. The program next prompts the user for the factor prices and factor shares of the variable inputs, the quantity and social price of the fixed input, and initial total variable costs. Thereafter the user is asked to input the elasticity of substitution for each variable input pair and the elasticity of each variable input demand with respect to each fixed input.

At this point, the program calculates the parameters of the translog restricted cost function and starts an iterative loop in which the user can conduct simulations using the initial or alternative technologies.

The loop begins by asking the user whether a simulation is to be conducted under the initial conditions or altered conditions, or if the user is finished. If the user wants to alter the initial conditions, there is an option for complete reentry of initial conditions and another for only partial alterations in the initial conditions.

If a simulation is desired, the user is offered three options for setting the benefits to be received by the firm from the subsidy scheme. First, the benefits may be declared by the user. Second, the user can permit the benefits to be determined by providing the program with a specific subsidy scheme for analysis. Such a subsidy scheme can alter any number of variable input prices or fixed input quantities. Third, the user can select the benefit level used in the immediately preceding simulation if the current simulation is not the first.

If the user chooses to declare the benefit level directly, the program asks the user which *one* variable input price or fixed input quantity is to be altered to yield the benefits. If the user chooses to provide a subsidy scheme that implicitly determines benefits, the program asks the user to input the subsidized levels of variable input prices and fixed input quantities.

At this point, the program calculates benefits of subsidy levels, subsidized factor uses and shadow prices, deadweight losses, and a variety of measures of possible interest to the analyst. These outputs are then written out by the program. The program then returns to the top of the loop by querying the user as to whether or not another simulation is desired.

The inputs to the program are read from logical file number 5. The prompts are written on logical unit 6. The program output is written on logical unit 4. By anticipating what input the program will ask for—and in what order—the user can use cards or card images on a disk or tape to input the needed data in batch mode; the data will be read from logical file 5. In interactive mode, the console output file should be assigned logical file 5.

```
C
C
C                LOCATION POLICY SIMULATION MODEL
C
      COMMON/QUANT/Q
      JSTRNM=0
  888 JSTRNM=JSTRNM+1
      CALL VARNUM(JSTRNM,NV,NF)
      CALL INIT
      CALL INPUT(NV,NF)
      CALL SETPAR(NV,NF)
C     CALL CHECK(NV,NF)
      CALL BSCVAL(NV,NF)
      CALL WRBSVL(NV,NF)
      DO   100 ISMNM=1,100
      CALL SMSTR(LPTION,ISMNM,JSTRNM,NV,NF)
      IF(LPTION.EQ.0)GO TO 999
      IF(LPTION.EQ.2)GO TO 888
      WRITE(4,7)ISMNM,JSTRNM
    7 FORMAT(1H ,/,/,/,/,/,1H ,'              SIMULATION NUMBER',I3,1X,
     1               '; COST STRUCTURE NUMBER',I3)
      CALL TOL
      CALL BENSET(ISMNM,NV,NF,JNEGSH)
      IF(JNEGSH.EQ.1)GO TO 99
      CALL DWLC(NV,NF)
      CALL PQCHGS(ISMNM,NV,NF)
C     CALL CHECK2
   99 CONTINUE
  100 CONTINUE
  999 CONTINUE
      STOP
      END

      SUBROUTINE VARNUM(J,NV,NF)
      WRITE(4,3)J
    3 FORMAT(1H ,/,/,/,/,/,1H ,
     1 '              COST STRUCTURE NUMBER',I3,1X,'FOLLOWS.')
      WRITE(6,1)
    1 FORMAT(1H ,/,/,/,/,/,/,1H ,'INPUT NUMBER OF VARIABLE INPUTS AS "0#"',
     1       /,1H ,'INPUT NUMBER OF FIXED INPUTS AS "0#"',/,
     2          1H ,'MAX OF FORMER IS 05 , OF LATTER 02')
      READ(5,2) NV,NF
    2 FORMAT(2I2)
      RETURN
      END
```

```
      SUBROUTINE SMSTR(LPTION,I,J,NV,NF)
      WRITE(6,5)I,J
   5  FORMAT(1H ,/,1H ,'     IF YOU WANT TO CONDUCT SIMULATION NUMBER',
   1          I3,/,1H ,'     FOR COST STRUCTURE NUMBER',I3,/,1H ,
   2                  '           TYPE 1',/,1H ,
   3                  '     IF YOU ARE FINISHED',/,1H ,
   4                  '          TYPE 0',/,1H ,
   5      '    IF YOU WANT TO FULLY RESPECIFY THE COST STRUCTURE,',/,1H ,
   6                  '          TYPE 2',/,1H ,
   7         '    IF YOU TO ALTER THE COST STRUCTURE OR WANT',/,
   8   1H ,'    ANOTHER SET OF PRICES OR QUANTITIES',/,
   9                  '          TYPE 3')
      READ(5,6)LPTION
   6  FORMAT(I1)
      IF(LPTION.EQ.3)CALL NWVAR(NV,NF)
      RETURN
      END


      SUBROUTINE NWVAR(NV,NF)
      COMMON/QUANT/Q
      COMMON/PSNQS/PV(5),PF(2),SHR(5),XF(2),BFF0(3),FQ0(2),H0(2),ZQ
      WRITE(6,31)
  31  FORMAT(1H0,/,/,1H ,'IF YOU WANT A NEW QUANTITY OF OUTPUT',
   1          /,1H ,' TYPE 1 ;OTHERWISE TYPE ZERO')
      READ(5,32)INDEX
  32  FORMAT(I1)
      IF(INDEX.EQ.0)GO TO 50
      WRITE(6,33)I
  33  FORMAT(1H0,/,1H ,'TYPE NEW QUANTITY OF OUTPUT',I2)
      READ(5,34)Q
  34  FORMAT(F12.3)
  50  CONTINUE
      WRITE(6,20)
  20  FORMAT(1H0,'IF YOU WANT TO CHANGE SOME VARIABLE PRICE, TYPE 1;',
   1          /,1H ,'OTHERWISE, TYPE 0')
      READ(5,2)INDEX
      IF(INDEX.NE.1)GO TO 101
      DO 100 I=1,NV
      WRITE(6,1)I
   1  FORMAT(1H0,/,/,1H ,'IF YOU WANT A NEW PRICE FOR VARIABLE INPUT',
   1          I2,' TYPE 1 ;OTHERWISE TYPE ZERO')
      READ(5,2)INDEX
   2  FORMAT(I1)
      IF(INDEX.EQ.0)GO TO 100
      WRITE(6,3)I
   3  FORMAT(1H0,/,1H ,'TYPE NEW PRICE FOR VARIABLE INPUT',I2)
      READ(5,4)PV(I)
   4  FORMAT(F12.3)
 100  CONTINUE
 101  CONTINUE
```

```
      IF(NF.LT.1)GO TO 301
      WRITE(6,21)
21    FORMAT(1H0,'IF YOU WANT TO CHANGE SOME FIXED QUANTITY, TYPE 1;',
     1           /,1H ,'OTHERWISE, TYPE 0')
      READ(5,2)INDEX
      IF(INDEX.NE.1)GO TO 201
      DO 200 I=1,NF
      WRITE(6,5)I
5     FORMAT(1H0,/,/,1H ,'IF YOU WANT A NEW QUANTITY FOR FIXED INPUT',
     1           I2,' TYPE 1 ;OTHERWISE TYPE ZERO')
      READ(5,6)INDEX
6     FORMAT(I1)
      IF(INDEX.EQ.0)GO TO 200
      WRITE(6,7)I
7     FORMAT(1H0,/,1H ,'TYPE NEW QUANTITY FOR FIXED INPUT',I2)
      READ(5,8)XF(I)
8     FORMAT(F12.3)
200   CONTINUE
201   CONTINUE
      WRITE(6,22)
22    FORMAT(1H0,'IF YOU WANT TO CHANGE SOME FIXED INPUT PRICE, TYPE 1;'
     1           /,1H ,'OTHERWISE, TYPE 0')
      READ(5,2)INDEX
      IF(INDEX.NE.1)GO TO 301
      DO 300 I=1,NF
      WRITE(6,9)I
9     FORMAT(1H0,/,/,1H ,'IF YOU WANT A NEW PRICE FOR FIXED INPUT',
     1           I2,' TYPE 1 ;OTHERWISE TYPE ZERO')
      READ(5,12)INDEX
12    FORMAT(I1)
      IF(INDEX.EQ.0)GO TO 300
      WRITE(6,13)I
13    FORMAT(1H0,/,1H ,'TYPE NEW PRICE FOR FIXED INPUT',I2)
      READ(5,14)PF(I)
14    FORMAT(F12.3)
300   CONTINUE
301   CONTINUE
      WRITE(4,15)
15    FORMAT(/,/,/,1H ,'*********************************************',
     1       /,/,1H ,'                  NEW ECONOMIC VARIABLES',/,1H ,
     2       '                  AND/OR COST STRUCTURE.',/,/,/,
     3           1H ,'     FOLLOWING HOLD UNTIL FURTHER NOTICE',
     4       /,/,1H ,'*********************************************')
      CALL BSCVAL(NV,NF)
      CALL WRBSVL(NV,NF)
      WRITE(6,30)
30    FORMAT(1H,/,1H ,'IF YOU WANT SOME CHANGE IN TECHNOLOGY, TYPE 1;',
     1           /,1H ,'OTHERWISE TYPE 0')
      READ(5,32)INDEX
      IF(INDEX.EQ.1)CALL TECSET(NV,NF)
      RETURN
      END
```

```
      SUBROUTINE INIT
      COMMON/BEN/BNFTS
      COMMON/QUANT/Q
      COMMON/PSNQS/PV(5),PF(2),SHR(5),XF(2),BFF0(3),FQ0(2),H0(2),ZQ
      COMMON/ELASS/ESOREL(5,5),ELASVV(5,5),ELASVF(5,2)
      COMMON/CS/BASE,A(5),H(2),AVV(5,5),GVF(5,2),BFF(2,2),TVQ(5),THFQ(2)
     1              ,SMSHEL(2)
      COMMON/BSVL/BY(5),BW(2),BCOST,SCOST,BFXCST
      COMMON/SUBPQS/SUBPV(5),SUBXF(2),SW(2),SY(5)
      Q=0.0
      BNFTS=0.0
      BCOST=0.0
      BFXCST=0.0
      DO 100 I=1,5
      BY(I)=0.0
      SY(I)=0.0
      SUBPV(I)=0.0
      PV(I)=0.0
      SHR(I)=0.0
      TVQ(I)=0.0
      A(I)=0.0
      DO 10 J=1,5
      ESOREL(I,J)=0.0
      ELASVV(I,J)=0.0
      AVV(I,J)=0.0
   10 CONTINUE
      DO 20 J=1,2
      GVF(I,J)=0.0
      ELASVF(I,J)=0.0
   20 CONTINUE
  100 CONTINUE
      DO 200 I=1,3
      BFF0(I)=0.0
  200 CONTINUE
      DO 300 I=1,2
      XF(I)=0.0
      PF(I)=0.0
      FQ0(I)=0.0
      THFQ(I)=0.0
      BW(I)=0.0
      SW(I)=0.0
      SUBXF(I)=0.0
      H(I)=0.0
      H0(I)=0.0
      DO 45 J=1,2
      BFF(I,J)=0.0
   45 CONTINUE
  300 CONTINUE
      RETURN
      END
```

```
      SUBROUTINE INPUT(NV,NF)
      COMMON/QUANT/Q
      COMMON/PSNQS/PV(5),PF(2),SHR(5),XF(2),BFF0(3),FQO(2),H0(2),ZQ
      COMMON/ELASS/ESOREL(5,5),ELASVV(5,5),ELASVF(5,2)
      COMMON/CS/BASE,A(5),H(2),AVV(5,5),GVF(5,2),BFF(2,2),TVQ(5),THFQ(2)
     1                ,SMSHEL(2)
      WRITE(6,2)
    2 FORMAT(/,/,1H ,'INPUT QUANTITY. USE DECIMAL POINTS IN ALL INPUTS')
      READ(5,3)Q
    3 FORMAT(F12.2)
      WRITE(4,2)
      WRITE(4,33)Q
   33 FORMAT(1H ,F12.2)
      DO 100 I=1,NV
      WRITE(6,31)I
   31 FORMAT(1H0,'INPUT PRICE OF VARIABLE INPUT',3X,I2)
      READ(5,4)PV(I)
      WRITE(6,32)I
   32 FORMAT(1H0,'INPUT SHARE OF VARIABLE INPUT',3X,I2)
      READ(5,4)SHR(I)
    4 FORMAT(F12.2)
      WRITE(4,31)I
      WRITE(4,44)PV(I)
      WRITE(4,32)I
      WRITE(4,44)SHR(I)
   44 FORMAT(1H ,F12.2)
  100 CONTINUE
      WRITE(6,16)
   16 FORMAT(1H0,'INPUT BASE COST LEVEL')
      READ(5,4)BASE
      WRITE(4,16)
      WRITE(4,44)BASE
      IF(NF.EQ.0)GO TO 201
      DO 200 I=1,NF
      WRITE(6,5)I
    5 FORMAT(1H0,'INPUT QUANTITY OF FIXED INPUT',3X,I2)
      READ(5,4)XF(I)
C     WRITE(6,6)I
C   6 FORMAT(1H0,'INPUT BFF0, OWN SQUARE COEFF, FOR FIXED INPUT',3X,I2)
C     READ(5,4)BFF0(I)
C     IF(I.LT.2)GO TO 69
C     WRITE(6,66)
C  66 FORMAT(1H0,'INPUT CROSS BFF0 FOR FIXED INPUTS',3X,I2)
C     READ(5,4)BFF0(3)
   69 CONTINUE
      WRITE(6,666)I
  666 FORMAT(1H0,'INPUT SOCIAL PRICE OF FIXED INPUT',3X,I2)
      READ(5,4)PF(I)
      WRITE(4,5)I
      WRITE(4,44)XF(I)
      WRITE(4,666)I
      WRITE(4,44)PF(I)
C     WRITE(4,6)I
C     WRITE(4,44)BFF0(I)
```

```
C       IF(I.LT.2)GO TO 70
C       WRITE(4,66)
C       WRITE(4,44)BFF0(3)
   70   CONTINUE
  200   CONTINUE
  201   CONTINUE
        NVM1=NV-1
        DO 300 I=1,NVM1
        II=I
        IP1=I+1
        IF(IP1.GT.NV)GO TO 400
        DO 300 J=IP1,NV
        JJ=J
        WRITE(6,9)I,J
    9   FORMAT(1H0,'INPUT ELAS. OF SUBST. FOR VARIABLE INPUTS',
       1                         1X,I2,1X,'AND',1X,I2,1X)
        READ(5,4)ELASVV(I,J)
        ELASVV(J,I)=ELASVV(I,J)
        WRITE(4,9)I,J
        WRITE(4,44)ELASVV(I,J)
  300   CONTINUE
  400   CONTINUE
        IF(NF.EQ.0)GO TO 501
        DO 500 I=1,NV
        DO 500 J=1,NF
        WRITE(6,10)I,J
   10   FORMAT(1H0,'INPUT ELAS. OF VARIABLE INPUT',1X,I2,1X,
       1         'WITH RESPECT TO FIXED INPUT',1X,I2)
        READ(5,4)ELASVF(I,J)
        WRITE(4,10)I,J
        WRITE(4,44)ELASVF(I,J)
  500   CONTINUE
  501   CONTINUE
        RETURN
        END


        SUBROUTINE SETPAR(NV,NF)
        COMMON/QUANT/Q
        COMMON/PSNQS/PV(5),PF(2),SHR(5),XF(2),BFF0(3),FQ0(2),H0(2),ZQ
        COMMON/ELASS/ESOREL(5,5),ELASVV(5,5),ELASVF(5,2)
        COMMON/CS/BASE,A(5),H(2),AVV(5,5),GVF(5,2),BFF(2,2),TVQ(5),THFQ(2)
       1         ,SMSHEL(2)
C*****************************************************************
C                    SET AVV FOR I NE J
C*****************************************************************
        NVM1=NV-1
        DO 100 I=1,NVM1
        IP1=I+1
        DO 100 J=IP1,NV
        AVV(I,J)=ELASVV(I,J)*(SHR(I)*SHR(J))-SHR(I)*SHR(J)
        AVV(J,I)=AVV(I,J)
  100   CONTINUE
        IF(NF.EQ.0)GO TO 281
```

```
C*********************************************************************
C                   SET GVF USING INITIAL SHADOW SHARES
C*********************************************************************
      NVM1=NV-1
      DO 250 J=1,NF
      SUMGVF=0.
      SMSHEL(J)=0.
      DO 150 K=1,NV
      SMSHEL(J)=SMSHEL(J) + SHR(K)*ELASVF(K,J)
  150 CONTINUE
      DO 200 I=1,NVM1
      GVF(I,J)=SHR(I)*ELASVF(I,J)-SMSHEL(J)*SHR(I)
      SUMGVF=SUMGVF+GVF(I,J)
  200 CONTINUE
      GVF(NV,J)=-SUMGVF
      BFF(J,J)=-(SMSHEL(J)**2)
  250 CONTINUE
C*********************************************************************
C                              SET TVQ
C*********************************************************************
      DO 280 I=1,NVM1
      SMGVFF=0.0
      DO 275 J=1,NF
      SMGVFF=SMGVFF+GVF(I,J)
  275 CONTINUE
      TVQ(I)=-SMGVFF
  280 CONTINUE
  281 CONTINUE
      SUMTVQ=0.0
      DO 290 I=1,NVM1
  290 SUMTVQ=SUMTVQ+TVQ(I)
      TVQ(NV)=-SUMTVQ
C*********************************************************************
C                          SET AVV FOR I=J
C*********************************************************************
      DO 400 I=1,NV
      SUMAVV=0
      DO 300 J=1,NV
      IF(J.NE.I)SUMAVV=SUMAVV+AVV(I,J)
  300 CONTINUE
      AVV(I,I)=-SUMAVV
  400 CONTINUE
C*********************************************************************
C                            SET A(V)
C*********************************************************************
      DO 500 I=1,NV
      SUMVVP=0
      SUMVFX=0
      DO 450 J=1,NV
  450 SUMVVP=SUMVVP+AVV(I,J)*LOG(PV(J))
      IF(NF.EQ.0)GO TO 476
      DO 475 K=1,NF
      SUMVFX=SUMVFX+GVF(I,K)*LOG(XF(K))
  475 CONTINUE
```

```
  476 CONTINUE
      A(I)=( SHR(I)-SUMVVP -SUMVFX ) - LOG(Q)*TVQ(I)
  500 CONTINUE
      IF(NF.EQ.0)GO TO 4501
C*********************************************************************
C                            SET BFF
C*********************************************************************
      DO 3000 I=1,NF
      IF(I.EQ.1)GO TO 1000
      BFF(1,2)=0
      BFF(2,1)=0
C     BFF(2,2)=BFF0(2)
C     GO TO 2000
 1000 CONTINUE
C     BFF(1,1)=BFF0(1)
C2000 CONTINUE
 3000 CONTINUE
C*********************************************************************
C                            SET THFQ
C*********************************************************************
      DO 4000 I=1,NF
      SUMBFF=0.0
      DO 3500 J=1,NF
      SUMBFF=SUMBFF+BFF(I,J)
 3500 CONTINUE
      THFQ(I)=-SUMBFF
 4000 CONTINUE
C*********************************************************************
C                            SET H(F)
C*********************************************************************
      DO 4500 I=1,NF
      SMGVF=0.
      SMBFF=0.
      DO 4100 J=I,NV
      SMGVF=SMGVF+GVF(J,I)*LOG(PV(J))
 4100 CONTINUE
      DO 4200 J=1,NF
      SMBFF=SMBFF+BFF(I,J)*LOG(XF(J))
 4200 CONTINUE
      H(I)=SMSHEL(I)-SMBFF-SMGVF-THFQ(I)*LOG(Q)
 4500 CONTINUE
 4501 CONTINUE
C*********************************************************************
C              SET ZQ ( COEFFICIENT OF LOG(Q) )
C*********************************************************************
      SUMH=0.
      IF(NF.LT.1)GO TO 4506
      DO 4505 I=1,NF
      SUMH=SUMH+H(I)
 4505 CONTINUE
 4506 CONTINUE
      ZQ=1-SUMH
```

```
C************************************************************************
C                     SET BASE (CONSTANT TERM)
C************************************************************************
      SV=0.
      SF=0.
      SVV=0.
      SVF=0.
      SFF=0.
      SVQ=0.
      SFQ=0.
      DO 5000 I=1,NV
      SV=SV+A(I)*LOG(PV(I))
      SVQ=SVQ+TVQ(I)*LOG(Q)*LOG(PV(I))
      DO 4600 J=1,NV
      SVV=SVV+.5*AVV(I,J)*LOG(PV(I))*LOG(PV(J))
 4600 CONTINUE
      IF(NF.EQ.0)GO TO 4701
      DO 4700 K=1,NF
      SVF=SVF+GVF(I,K)*LOG(PV(I))*LOG(XF(K))
      IF(I.GT.1)GO TO 4700
      SFQ=SFQ+THFQ(K)*LOG(XF(K))*LOG(Q)
      SF=SF+H(K)*LOG(XF(K))
      DO 4650 L=1,NF
      SFF=SFF+.5*BFF(K,L)*LOG(XF(K))*LOG(XF(L))
 4650 CONTINUE
 4700 CONTINUE
 4701 CONTINUE
 5000 CONTINUE
      BASE=LOG(BASE)-SV-SF-SVV-SVF-SFF-SVQ-SFQ-ZQ*LOG(Q)
      CALL TECH
      RETURN
      END

      SUBROUTINE BSCVAL(NV,NF)
      COMMON/QUANT/Q
      COMMON/PSNQS/PV(5),PF(2),SHR(5),XF(2),BFF0(3),FQ0(2),H0(2),ZQ
      COMMON/CS/BASE,A(5),H(2),AVV(5,5),GVF(5,2),BFF(2,2),TVQ(5),THFQ(2)
     1        ,SMSHEL(2)
      COMMON/BSVL/BY(5),BW(2),BCOST,SCOST,BFXCST
C************************************************************************
C                     CHECK FOR A GIFFEN GOOD
C************************************************************************
      ICALL=-1
      IG=0
      CALL GIFCHK(NV,NF,ICALL,IG,SUBPVL,SUBPVH)
      IF(IG.EQ.0)GO TO 1
      IF(IG.EQ.1)RETURN
      WRITE(4,2)
    2 FORMAT(1H ,'BASIC VALUES INCLUDE MULTIPLE GIFFEN EFFECTS')
```

```
C***********************************************************************
C                         INITIALIZE
C***********************************************************************
   1    BFXCST=0.0
        SUMLV1=0.0
        SUMLF1=0.0
        SUM1=0.0
        SUM2=0.0
        SUM3=0.0
        SUM4=0.0
        SUM5=0.0
C***********************************************************************
C                 ACCUMULATE PARTS OF COST FUNCTION
C***********************************************************************
        DO 200 I=1,NV
        SUMLV1=SUMLV1+A(I)*LOG(PV(I))
        DO 100 J=1,NV
 100    SUM1=SUM1+.5*AVV(I,J)*LOG(PV(I))*LOG(PV(J))
        IF(NF.EQ.0)GO TO 151
        DO 150 K=1,NF
        SUM2=SUM2+GVF(I,K)*LOG(PV(I))*LOG(XF(K))
 150    CONTINUE
 151    CONTINUE
        SUM3=SUM3+TVQ(I)*LOG(PV(I))*LOG(Q)
 200    CONTINUE
        IF(NF.EQ.0)GO TO 401
        DO 400 I=1,NF
        SUMLF1=SUMLF1+H(I)*LOG(XF(I))
        DO 300 J=1,NF
 300    SUM4=SUM4+.5*BFF(I,J)*LOG(XF(I))*LOG(XF(J))
        SUM5=SUM5+THFQ(I)*LOG(XF(I))*LOG(Q)
 400    CONTINUE
 401    CONTINUE
C***********************************************************************
C                    COMPUTE LOG COST & COST
C***********************************************************************
        BLGCST=SUM1+SUM2+SUM3+SUM4+SUM5+SUMLV1+SUMLF1+BASE+ZQ*LOG(Q)
        BCOST=EXP(BLGCST)
C***********************************************************************
C                 COMPUTE VARIABLE INPUT DEMANDS
C***********************************************************************
        DO 700 I=1,NV
        SSUM1=0.0
        SSUM2=0.0
        DO 500 J=1,NV
 500    SSUM1=SSUM1+AVV(I,J)*LOG(PV(J))
        IF(NF.EQ.0)GO TO 601
        DO 600 K=1,NF
        SSUM2=SSUM2+GVF(I,K)*LOG(XF(K))
 600    CONTINUE
 601    CONTINUE
        BY(I)=(BCOST/PV(I))*(A(I)+SSUM1+SSUM2+TVQ(I)*LOG(Q))
 700    CONTINUE
        IF(NF.EQ.0)GO TO 1101
```

```
C***********************************************************************
C                  COMPUTE FIXED INPUT SHADOW PRICES
C***********************************************************************
      DO 1000 I=1,NF
      SSSUM1=0.0
      SSSUM2=0.0
      DO 800 J=1,NV
 800  SSSUM1=SSSUM1+GVF(J,I)*LOG(PV(J))
      DO 900 K=1,NF
 900  SSSUM2=SSSUM2+BFF(I,K)*LOG(XF(K))
      BW(I)=-1.*(BCOST/XF(I))*(H(I)+SSSUM1+SSSUM2+THFQ(I)*LOG(Q))
1000  CONTINUE
C***********************************************************************
C                  COMPUTE FIXED COST AT SOCIAL PRICES
C***********************************************************************
      DO 1100 I=1,NF
      BFXCST=PF(I)*XF(I)+BFXCST
1100  CONTINUE
1101  CONTINUE
      RETURN
      END


      SUBROUTINE WRBSVL(NV,NF)
      COMMON/QUANT/Q
      COMMON/PSNQS/PV(5),PF(2),SHR(5),XF(2),BFF0(3),FQ0(2),H0(2),ZQ
      COMMON/BSVL/BY(5),BW(2),BCOST,SCOST,BFXCST
      WRITE(4,1)Q,BCOST
 1    FORMAT(/,1H ,'FIRM OUTPUT=',F12.3,/1H ,'INITIAL COST=',F11.3)
      DO 100 I=1,NV
      WRITE(4,2)I,BY(I)
 2    FORMAT(1H ,/,/,1H ,'INITIAL DEMAND FOR VARIABLE INPUT',
     1            I2,2X,'=',F12.3)
      WRITE(4,4)I,PV(I)
 4    FORMAT(1H ,'INITIAL PRICE FOR VARIABLE INPUT',I2,2X,'=',F12.3)
 100  CONTINUE
      IF(NF.EQ.0)GO TO 201
      DO 200 J=1,NF
      WRITE(4,3)J,BW(J)
 3    FORMAT(1H ,/1H ,'INITIAL SHADOW VALUE OF FIXED INPUT',I2,2X,'=',
     1            F12.3)
      WRITE(4,5)J,XF(J)
 5    FORMAT(1H ,'INITIAL QUANTITY FOR FIXED INPUT',I2,2X,'=',F12.3)
      WRITE(4,6)J,PF(J)
 6    FORMAT(1H ,'INITIAL SOCIAL PRICE FOR FIXED INPUT',I2,2X,'=',F12.3)
 200  CONTINUE
 201  CONTINUE
      RETURN
      END
```

```
      SUBROUTINE TOL
      COMMON/TOL1/TOLER
      TOLER=.0001
C     WRITE(6,1)
1     FORMAT(1H0,/,/,1H ,'DO YOU WANT THE DEFAULT TOLERANCE THAT',/,
     1            1H ,'YIELDS BENEFITS WITHIN 1/2 PERCENT OF',/,
     2            1H ,'BENEFITS SPECIFIED FOR SIMULATION?',/,
     3            1H ,'IF YES, TYPE 1; OTHERWISE TYPE 0.')
C     READ(5,2)J
2     FORMAT(I1)
C     IF(J.EQ.1)GO TO 100
C     WRITE(6,3)
3     FORMAT(/,1H ,'ENTER THE DESIRED TOLERANCE AS A DECIMAL FRACTION',
     1       /,1H ,'EG., .005 IS THE DEFAULT LEVEL YOU HAVE REJECTED')
C     READ(5,4)TOLER
C4    FORMAT(F6.3)
C     TOLERP=100*TOLER
C100  WRITE(4,5)TOLERP
5     FORMAT(1H ,/,/,1H ,'ESTIMATES OF BENEFITS WILL BE WITHIN ',F4.2,
     1              2X,'PERCENT OF SPECIFIED BENEFIT LEVEL')
      RETURN
      END


      SUBROUTINE BENSET(NUM,NV,NF,JNEGSH)
      COMMON/BEN/BNFTS
      IF(NUM.GT.1)WRITE(6,10)
10    FORMAT(1H0,/,1H ,'IF YOU WANT SAME BENEFITS AS LAST',/,1H ,
     1               'SIMULATION FOR THIS COST STUCTURE',/,1H ,
     2               'TYPE 1')
      WRITE(6,11)
11    FORMAT(1H ,'IF YOU WANT TO SET A NEW BENEFIT LEVEL',/,1H ,
     1            'TYPE 2')
      WRITE(6,12)
12    FORMAT(1H ,'IF YOU WANT BENEFIT LEVEL SET BY THE SCHEME',/,1H ,
     1            'TYPE 3')
      READ(5,13)LPTBEN
13    FORMAT(I1)
      IF(LPTBEN.NE.2)GO TO 3
      WRITE(6,14)
14    FORMAT(1H ,/,1H ,'INPUT LEVEL OF BENEFITS')
      READ(5,15)BNFTS
15    FORMAT(F12.2)
3     IF(LPTBEN.NE.3)WRITE(4,16)BNFTS,NUM
16    FORMAT(1H ,/,/,/,1H ,'          BENEFITS=',F12.2,2X,'IN SCHEME',I3)
C     CALL CHECK2
      JNEGSH=0
      IF(LPTBEN.NE.3)CALL BINSR(NV,NF,JNEGSH)
      IF(LPTBEN.EQ.3)CALL SUBBEN(NUM,NV,NF)
      RETURN
      END
```

```
      SUBROUTINE BINSR(NV,NF,JNEGSH)
      COMMON/SUBIND/JSUBV,JSUBF
      COMMON/BEN/BNFTS
      COMMON/QUANT/Q
      COMMON/TOL1/TOLER
      COMMON/PSNQS/PV(5),PF(2),SHR(5),XF(2),BFF0(3),FQ0(2),H0(2),ZQ
      COMMON/CS/BASE,A(5),H(2),AVV(5,5),GVF(5,2),BFF(2,2),TVQ(5),THFQ(2)
     1           ,SMSHEL(2)
      COMMON/BSVL/BY(5),BW(2),BCOST,SCOST,BFXCST
      COMMON/SUBPQS/SUBPV(5),SUBXF(2),SW(2),SY(5)
      JSUBF=0
      WRITE(6,1)
    1 FORMAT(1H0,'TYPE INTEGER OF VARIABLE INPUT TO SUBSIDIZE.',/,1H ,
     1           'IF SUBSIDIZING FIXED INPUT, TYPE 0')
      READ(5,2)JSUBV
    2 FORMAT(I1)
      IF(JSUBV.GT.0)WRITE(4,3)JSUBV
    3 FORMAT(1H ,/1H ,'SCHEME SUBSIDIZES VARIABLE INPUT',I2)
      IF(JSUBV.GT.0)GO TO 10
      WRITE(6,4)
    4 FORMAT(1H0,'TYPE INTEGER OF FIXED INPUT TO SUBSIDIZE')
      READ(5,2)JSUBF
      WRITE(4,5)JSUBF
    5 FORMAT(1H ,/1H ,'SCHEME SUBSIDIZES FIXED INPUT',I2)
      IF(BW(JSUBF).GT.0)GO TO 10
      WRITE(6,7)JSUBF
      WRITE(4,7)JSUBF
    7 FORMAT(1H0,/,1H ,'FIXED INPUT',I2,2X,'HAS A NEGATIVE SHADOW',
     1               ' PRICE; INCREMENTS YIELD NO BENEFITS')
      JNEGSH=1
      RETURN
   10 CONTINUE
C**********************************************************************
C
C            SET INITIAL BOUNDS FOR SUBSIDIZED PRICE
C                    OF VARIABLE INPUT
C
C**********************************************************************
      DO 20 I=1,NV
   20 SUBPV(I)=PV(I)
      IF(NF.EQ.0)GO TO 31
      DO 30 J=1,NF
      SUBXF(J)=XF(J)
   30 CONTINUE
   31 CONTINUE
      IQUERY=0
      IF(JSUBF.GT.0)GO TO 90
      SUBPVL=PV(JSUBV)-BNFTS/BY(JSUBV)
      SUBPVH=PV(JSUBV)
      IF(SUBPVL.GT.0)GO TO 98
```

```
C*********************************************************************
C            CHECK IF BENEFITS POTENTIALLY TOO BIG FOR
C                  THIS VARIABLE INPUT
C*********************************************************************
      SUBPVL=.0001
      SUBPV(JSUBV)=.1*SUBPVL+.9*SUBPVH
      ICALL=JSUBV
      CALL GIFCHK(NV,NF,ICALL,IG,SUBPVL,SUBPVH)
      IF(IG.EQ.1)RETURN
      IQUERY=1
      GO TO 98
 90   CONTINUE
C*********************************************************************
C            SET INITIAL CONDITIONAL BOUNDS FOR SUBSIDIZED
C                  QUANTITY OF FIXED INPUT
C*********************************************************************
      XFMULT=10.
      SUBXFL=XF(JSUBF)+BNFTS/BW(JSUBF)
      SUBXFH=XF(JSUBF)+(BNFTS+XFMULT*BCOST)/BW(JSUBF)
C*********************************************************************
C            CHECK INITIAL UPPER BOUND ON SUBSIDIZED
C                  FIXED INPUT QUANTITY
C                  AND REVISE IF NECESSARY
C*********************************************************************
      XFMLTO=XFMULT
      CALL HSBXFC(NV,NF,SUBXFH,JSUBF,XFMULT,JNEGSH)
      IF(JNEGSH.EQ.1)RETURN
 95   RATIO=XFMULT/XFMLTO
      IF(RATIO.LT.5)GO TO 98
      SUBXFH=XF(JSUBF)+(BNFTS+XFMULT*BCOST)/BW(JSUBF)
      IF(JNEGSH.EQ.1)RETURN
      CALL HSBXFC(NV,NF,SUBXFH,JSUBF,XFMULT,JNEGSH)
      GO TO 95
C*********************************************************************
C                  INITIALIZE VARIABLES FOR CHECKING
C                  INCREASINGNESS OF COST FUNCTION
C                  IN PRICES AND 1/(FIXED INPUTS)
C*********************************************************************
 98   ITER=0
      SCOSTL=0.
      PUP=0.
 99   CONTINUE
      ITER=ITER+1
      IF(IQUERY.EQ.1.AND.ITER.EQ.1)GO TO 100
C*********************************************************************
C            GUESS SUBSIDIZED PRICE OR QUANTITY
C                  AND CHECK FOR GIFFEN EFFECTS
C*********************************************************************
      IF(JSUBV.EQ.0)GO TO 1234
      SUBPV(JSUBV)= .5*(SUBPVH+SUBPVL)
      ICALL=JSUBV
      CALL GIFCHK(NV,NF,ICALL,IG,SUBPVL,SUBPVH)
      IF(IG.EQ.1 .AND. ICALL.EQ.0)JNEGSH=1
      IF(IG.EQ.1)RETURN
```

```
1234 IF(JSUBV.EQ.0)SUBXF(JSUBF)=.5*(SUBXFH+SUBXFL)
C*************************************************************************
C                  INITIALIZE PARTS OF COST FUNCTION
C*************************************************************************
 100  SUMLV1=0.0
      SUMLF1=0.0
      SUM1=0.0
      SUM2=0.0
      SUM3=0.0
      SUM4=0.0
      SUM5=0.0
C*************************************************************************
C                  COMPUTE PARTS OF COST FUNCTION
C*************************************************************************
      DO 200 I=1,NV
      SUMLV1=SUMLV1+A(I)*LOG(SUBPV(I))
      DO 110 J=1,NV
      SUM1=SUM1+.5*AVV(I,J)*LOG(SUBPV(I))*LOG(SUBPV(J))
 110  CONTINUE
      IF(NF.EQ.0)GO TO 151
      DO 150 K=1,NF
      SUM2=SUM2+GVF(I,K)*LOG(SUBPV(I))*LOG(SUBXF(K))
 150  CONTINUE
 151  CONTINUE
      SUM3=SUM3+TVQ(I)*LOG(SUBPV(I))*LOG(Q)
 200  CONTINUE
      IF(NF.EQ.0)GO TO 401
      DO 400 I=1,NF
      SUMLF1=SUMLF1+H(I)*LOG(SUBXF(I))
      DO 300 J=1,NF
 300  SUM4=SUM4+.5*BFF(I,J)*LOG(SUBXF(I))*LOG(SUBXF(J))
      SUM5=SUM5+THFQ(I)*LOG(SUBXF(I))*LOG(Q)
 400  CONTINUE
 401  CONTINUE
C*************************************************************************
C                  COMPUTE LOG COST & COST
C                  AND ASSOCIATED BENEFIT LEVEL
C*************************************************************************
      SLGCST=SUM1+SUM2+SUM3+SUM4+SUM5+SUMLV1+SUMLF1+BASE+ZQ*LOG(Q)
      SCOST=EXP(SLGCST)
      BENGS=BCOST-SCOST
C*************************************************************************
C                  CHECK INCREASINGNESS OF
C                  COST FUNCTION
C*************************************************************************

      IF(ITER.EQ.1.AND.BENGS.LT.0)WRITE(6,6)ITER
      IF(ITER.EQ.1.AND.BENGS.LT.0)WRITE(4,6)ITER
 6    FORMAT(1H ,/1H ,'COSTS RISE AS PRICES FALL OR INPUT CANNOT YIELD',
     1' BENEFITS',/,1H ,'JOB SKIPS SCHEME; ITER=',I8,
     2    /,1H ,'TYPE 1 TO ACKNOWLEDGE PROBLEM')
      IF(ITER.EQ.1.AND.BENGS.LT.0)READ(5,83)KKK
 83   FORMAT(I1)
      IF(ITER.EQ.1.AND.BENGS.LT.0)JNEGSH=1
```

```
      IF(ITER.EQ.1.AND.BENGS.LT.0)RETURN
      DISCR=(ABS(BENGS-BNFTS))/BNFTS
      CHK=(SCOST-SCOSTL)*PUP
      IF(ITER.GT.1.AND.CHK.LT.0)WRITE(6,6)ITER
      IF(ITER.GT.1.AND.CHK.LT.0)WRITE(4,6)ITER
      IF(ITER.GT.1.AND.CHK.LT.0)READ(5,83)KKK
      IF(ITER.GT.1.AND.CHK.LT.0)JNEGSH=1
      IF(ITER.GT.1.AND.CHK.LT.0)RETURN
      SCOSTL=SCOST
C*************************************************************************
C                        CHECK BENEFIT GUESS FOR
C                        CLOSENESS TO NEEDED LEVEL
C*************************************************************************
      IF(DISCR.LT.TOLER)GO TO 499
      IF(JSUBV.EQ.0)GO TO 425
C*************************************************************************
C                        CHECK IF ZERO PRICE NOT
C                        ENOUGH TO YIELD NEEEDED LEVEL
C*************************************************************************
      IIQ=0
      IF(IQUERY.EQ.1.AND.SUBPV(JSUBV).LT. .001)IIQ=1
      IF(IIQ.EQ.1)WRITE(4,66)
      IF(IIQ.EQ.1)WRITE(6,66)
      IF(IIQ.EQ.1)READ(5,83)KKK
      IF(IIQ.EQ.1)JNEGSH=1
      IF(IIQ.EQ.1)RETURN
   66 FORMAT(1H ,/1H ,'ZERO PRICE NOT ENOUGH TO YIELD BENEFIT LEVEL',
     1      /,1H ,'SKIP TO NEXT SCHEME; TYPE 1 TO ACKNOWLEDGE PROBLEM')
C*************************************************************************
C                        RESET BOUNDS ON
C                        SUBSIDIZED PRICE
C*************************************************************************
      IF(BENGS.GT.BNFTS)SUBPVL=SUBPV(JSUBV)
      IF(BENGS.GT.BNFTS)PUP=1.
      IF(BENGS.LE.BNFTS)SUBPVH=SUBPV(JSUBV)
      IF(BENGS.LE.BNFTS)PUP=-1.
      GO TO 99
  425 CONTINUE
C*************************************************************************
C                        RESET BOUNDS ON
C                        SUBSIDIZED QUANTITY
C*************************************************************************
      IF(BENGS.LE.BNFTS)SUBXFL=SUBXF(JSUBF)
      IF(BENGS.LE.BNFTS)PUP=-1.
      IF(BENGS.GT.BNFTS)SUBXFH=SUBXF(JSUBF)
      IF(BENGS.GT.BNFTS)PUP=1.0
      GO TO 99
  499 CONTINUE
      CALL SUBOUT(NV,NF)
      RETURN
      END
```

```
      SUBROUTINE HSBXFC(NV,NF,SUBXFH,JSUBF,XFMULT,JNEGSH)
      COMMON/BEN/BNFTS
      COMMON/QUANT/Q
      COMMON/PSNQS/PV(5),PF(2),SHR(5),XF(2),BFF0(3),FQ0(2),H0(2),ZQ
      COMMON/CS/BASE,A(5),H(2),AVV(5,5),GVF(5,2),BFF(2,2),TVQ(5),THFQ(2)
     1      ,SMSHEL(2)
      COMMON/BSVL/BY(5),BW(2),BCOST,SCOST,BFXCST
      COMMON/SUBPQS/SUBPV(5),SUBXF(2),SW(2),SY(5)
      COMMON/SSXFS/SSUBXF(2)
      DO 10 I=1,NF
  10  SSUBXF(I)=SUBXF(I)
      SSUBXF(JSUBF)=SUBXFH
      SUMLV1=0.0
      SUMLF1=0.0
      SUM1=0.0
      SUM2=0.0
      SUM3=0.0
      SUM4=0.0
      SUM5=0.0
      SV=0.
      SF=0.
      DO 200 I=1,NV
      SUMLV1=SUMLV1+A(I)*LOG(SUBPV(I))
      SV=SV+GVF(I,JSUBF)*LOG(SUBPV(I))
      DO 100 J=1,NV
 100  SUM1=SUM1+.5*AVV(I,J)*LOG(SUBPV(I))*LOG(SUBPV(J))
      DO 150 K=1,NF
 150  SUM2=SUM2+GVF(I,K)*LOG(SUBPV(I))*LOG(SSUBXF(K))
      SUM3=SUM3+TVQ(I)*LOG(SUBPV(I))*LOG(Q)
 200  CONTINUE
      DO 400 I=1,NF
      SUMLF1=SUMLF1+H(I)*LOG(SSUBXF(I))
      SF=SF+BFF(I,JSUBF)*LOG(SSUBXF(I))
      DO 300 J=1,NF
 300  SUM4=SUM4+.5*BFF(I,J)*LOG(SSUBXF(I))*LOG(SSUBXF(J))
      SUM5=SUM5+THFQ(I)*LOG(SSUBXF(I))*LOG(Q)
 400  CONTINUE
      SLGCST=SUM1+SUM2+SUM3+SUM4+SUM5+SUMLV1+SUMLF1+BASE+ZQ*LOG(Q)
      SCOST=EXP(SLGCST)
      BENGS=BCOST-SCOST
      IF(BENGS.GE.BNFTS)GO TO 500
      XFMULT=10*XFMULT
      SW(JSUBF)=-1.0*(SCOST/SSUBXF(JSUBF))*(H(JSUBF)+SV+SF
     1                       +THFQ(JSUBF)*LOG(Q))
      IF(SW(JSUBF).GT.0)GO TO 500
      WRITE(4,1)JSUBF
  1   FORMAT(1H ,/,1H ,'FIXED INPUT',I2,' CANNOT YIELD ENOUGH BENEFITS')
      JNEGSH=1
 500  CONTINUE
      RETURN
      END
```

```
      SUBROUTINE SUBOUT(NV,NF)
      COMMON/BEN/BNFTS
      COMMON/QUANT/Q
      COMMON/PSNQS/PV(5),PF(2),SHR(5),XF(2),BFF0(3),FQ0(2),H0(2),ZQ
      COMMON/CS/BASE,A(5),H(2),AVV(5,5),GVF(5,2),BFF(2,2),TVQ(5),THFQ(2)
     1             ,SMSHEL(2)
      COMMON/BSVL/BY(5),BW(2),BCOST,SCOST,BFXCST
      COMMON/SUBPQS/SUBPV(5),SUBXF(2),SW(2),SY(5)
C*******************************************************************
C                    COMPUTE SUBSIDIZED DEMANDS
C*******************************************************************
      DO 900 I=1,NV
      SSUM1=0.0
      SSUM2=0.0
      DO 500 J=1,NV
  500 SSUM1=SSUM1+AVV(I,J)*LOG(SUBPV(J))
      IF(NF.EQ.0)GO TO 601
      DO 600 K=1,NF
      SSUM2=SSUM2+GVF(I,K)*LOG(SUBXF(K))
  600 CONTINUE
  601 CONTINUE
      SY(I)=(SCOST/SUBPV(I))*(A(I)+SSUM1+SSUM2+TVQ(I)*LOG(Q))
      WRITE(4,602)I,SUBPV(I),SY(I)
  602 FORMAT(1H ,/1H ,'SUBSIDIZED PRICE FOR VARIABLE INPUT',I2,2X,'=',
     1 F12.2,//,1H ,'SUBSIDIZED QUANTITY OF THAT VARIABLE INPUT =',F12.3)
  900 CONTINUE
      IF(NF.EQ.0)GO TO 1001
C*******************************************************************
C                 COMPUTE SUBSIDIZED SHADOW PRICES
C*******************************************************************
      DO 1000 I=1,NF
      SSSUM1=0.0
      SSSUM2=0.0
      DO 800 J=1,NV
  800 SSSUM1=SSSUM1+GVF(J,I)*LOG(SUBPV(J))
      DO 950 K=1,NF
  950 SSSUM2=SSSUM2+BFF(I,K)*LOG(SUBXF(K))
      SW(I)=-1.*(SCOST/SUBXF(I))*(H(I)+SSSUM1+SSSUM2+THFQ(I)*LOG(Q))
      WRITE(4,701)I,SW(I),SUBXF(I)
  701 FORMAT(1H ,/1H ,'SUBSIDIZED SHADOW PRICE OF FIXED INPUT',I2,2X,
     1'=',F12.3,/,1H ,'SUBSIDIZED QUANTITY OF THAT FIXED INPUT =',F12.3)
 1000 CONTINUE
 1001 CONTINUE
C*******************************************************************
C               CHECK FOR UPWARD SLOPING FACTOR DEMANDS
C*******************************************************************
      DO 2000 I=1,NV
      SHTRM=( SUBPV(I)*SY(I)/SCOST)*((SUBPV(I)*SY(I)/SCOST)-1)
      CHQ=AVV(I,I)+SHTRM
      IF(CHQ.GT.0.)WRITE(4,2001)I
 2001 FORMAT(1H ,/,'VARIABLE INPUT',I2,' IS GIFFEN')
 2000 CONTINUE
      RETURN
      END
```

```
      SUBROUTINE SUBBEN(NUM,NV,NF)
      COMMON/SUBIND/JSUBV,JSUBF
      COMMON/BEN/BNFTS
      COMMON/QUANT/Q
      COMMON/PSNQS/PV(5),PF(2),SHR(5),XF(2),BFF0(3),FQ0(2),H0(2),ZQ
      COMMON/CS/BASE,A(5),H(2),AVV(5,5),GVF(5,2),BFF(2,2),TVQ(5),THFQ(2)
     1          ,SMSHEL(2)
      COMMON/BSVL/BY(5),BW(2),BCOST,SCOST,BFXCST
      COMMON/SUBPQS/SUBPV(5),SUBXF(2),SW(2),SY(5)
      COMMON/SSXFS/SSUBXF(2)
      JSUBV=0
      JSUBF=0
C**********************************************************************
C
C                    SET SUBSIDIZED PRICES AND
C                         QUANTITIES
C
C**********************************************************************
      DO 10 I=1,NV
      WRITE(6,1)I
    1 FORMAT(1H0,/,1H ,'IF VARIABLE INPUT',I2,2X,'IS TO BE SUBSIDIZED',
     1               /,1H ,'              TYPE 1; OTHERWISE TYPE 0')
      READ(5,2)INDEX
    2 FORMAT(I1)
      IF(INDEX.EQ.0)SUBPV(I)=PV(I)
      IF(INDEX.EQ.0)GO TO 10
      JSUBV=1
      WRITE(6,3)I
    3 FORMAT(1H0,/,1H ,'INPUT SUBSIDIZED PRICE FOR VARIABLE INPUT',I2)
      READ(5,4)SUBPV(I)
    4 FORMAT(F12.2)
   10 CONTINUE
      IF(NF.EQ.0)GO TO 21
      DO 20 I=1,NF
      WRITE(6,5)I
    5 FORMAT(1H0,/,1H ,'IF FIXED INPUT',I2,2X,'IS TO BE SUBSIDIZED',
     1               /,1H ,'              TYPE 1; OTHERWISE TYPE 0')
      READ(5,6)INDEX
    6 FORMAT(I1)
      IF(INDEX.EQ.0)SUBXF(I)=XF(I)
      IF(INDEX.EQ.0)GO TO 20
      IF(I.EQ.1)JSUBF=1
      IF(I.EQ.2 .AND. JSUBF.EQ.1)JSUBF=3
      IF(I.EQ.2 .AND. JSUBF.EQ.0)JSUBF=2
      WRITE(6,7)I
    7 FORMAT(1H0,/,1H ,'INPUT SUBSIDIZED QUANTITY FOR FIXED INPUT',I2)
      READ(5,8)SUBXF(I)
    8 FORMAT(F12.2)
   20 CONTINUE
   21 CONTINUE
```

```
C*********************************************************************
C                        CHECK FOR GIFFEN EFFECTS
C*********************************************************************
      ICALL=0
      CALL GIFCHK(NV,NF,ICALL,IG,SUBPVL,SUBPVH)
      IF(IG.EQ.1)RETURN
C*********************************************************************
C                        INITIALIZE ELEMENTS OF
C                            SUBSIDIZED COSTS
C*********************************************************************
      SUMLV1=0.0
      SUMLF1=0.0
      SUM1=0.0
      SUM2=0.0
      SUM3=0.0
      SUM4=0.0
      SUM5=0.0
C*********************************************************************
C                        COMPUTE ELEMENTS OF
C                            SUBSIDIZED COSTS
C*********************************************************************
      DO 200 I=1,NV
      SUMLV1=SUMLV1+A(I)*LOG(SUBPV(I))
      DO 100 J=1,NV
  100 SUM1=SUM1+.5*AVV(I,J)*LOG(SUBPV(I))*LOG(SUBPV(J))
      IF(NF.EQ.0)GO TO 151
      DO 150 K=1,NF
      SUM2=SUM2+GVF(I,K)*LOG(SUBPV(I))*LOG(SUBXF(K))
  150 CONTINUE
  151 CONTINUE
      SUM3=SUM3+TVQ(I)*LOG(SUBPV(I))*LOG(Q)
  200 CONTINUE
      IF(NF.EQ.0)GO TO 401
      DO 400 I=1,NF
      SUMLF1=SUMLF1+H(I)*LOG(SUBXF(I))
      DO 300 J=1,NF
  300 SUM4=SUM4+.5*BFF(I,J)*LOG(SUBXF(I))*LOG(SUBXF(J))
      SUM5=SUM5+THFQ(I)*LOG(SUBXF(I))*LOG(Q)
  400 CONTINUE
  401 CONTINUE
C*********************************************************************
C                        COMPUTE LOG COST, COST, & BENEFITS
C                                UNDER SUBSIDY
C*********************************************************************
      SLGCST=SUM1+SUM2+SUM3+SUM4+SUM5+SUMLV1+SUMLF1+BASE+ZQ*LOG(Q)
      SCOST=EXP(SLGCST)
      BENGS=BCOST-SCOST
      BNFTS=BENGS
      WRITE(4,16)BNFTS,NUM
   16 FORMAT(1H0,/,/,/,1H ,'            BENEFITS=',F12.2,2X,'IN SCHEME',I3)
      WRITE(6,16)BNFTS,NUM
      WRITE(4,98)
```

```
98   FORMAT(1H ,/,/,/,/,
    1    '                        THESE BENEFITS ARE FROM THE',/,1H ,
    2    '                        FOLLOWING SUBSIDY SCHEME')
     WRITE(4,97)
97   FORMAT(1H ,/)
     DO 30 I=1,NV
     WRITE(4,9)I,SUBPV(I)
9    FORMAT(1H ,/,1H ,'SUBSIDIZED PRICE FOR VARIABLE INPUT',I2,1X,
    1         '=',F12.2)
30   CONTINUE
     IF(NF.EQ.0)GO TO 41
     DO 40 I=1,NF
     WRITE(4,99)I,SUBXF(I)
99   FORMAT(1H ,/,1H ,'SUBSIDIZED QUANTITY FOR FIXED INPUT',I2,1X,'=',
    1         F12.2)
40   CONTINUE
41   CONTINUE
     CALL SUBOUT(NV,NF)
     RETURN
     END


     SUBROUTINE PQCHGS(NUM,NV,NF)
     COMMON/PSNQS/PV(5),PF(2),SHR(5),XF(2),BFF0(3),FQ0(2),H0(2),ZQ
     COMMON/BSVL/BY(5),BW(2),BCOST,SCOST,BFXCST
     COMMON/SUBPQS/SUBPV(5),SUBXF(2),SW(2),SY(5)
     COMMON/CHGS/PVCHG(5),XFCHG(2),SPXCHG(2),QVCHG(5),CSTCHG
     CSTCHG=100*(SCOST-BCOST)/BCOST
     WRITE(4,1)NUM,CSTCHG
1    FORMAT(1H ,/,/,/,1H ,'THE PERCENT CHANGE IN COSTS FOR SCHEME',I3,
    1         2X,'=',F8.3)
     WRITE(4,10)
10   FORMAT(1H ,/)
     DO 100 I=1,NV
     QVCHG(I)=100*(SY(I)-BY(I))/BY(I)
     PVCHG(I)=100*(SUBPV(I)-PV(I))/PV(I)
     WRITE(4,2)I,PVCHG(I)
2    FORMAT(1H ,/,1H ,'THE PERCENT CHANGE IN VARIABLE INPUT PRICE',I2,
    1             2X,'=',F8.3)
     WRITE(4,3)I,QVCHG(I)
3    FORMAT(1H ,'THE PERCENT CHANGE IN VARIABLE INPUT QUANTITY',
    1             I2,2X,'=',F9.3)
100  CONTINUE
     WRITE(4,10)
     IF(NF.EQ.0)GO TO 201
     DO 200 I=1,NF
     XFCHG(I)=100*(SUBXF(I)-XF(I))/XF(I)
     IF(BW(I).LT..00001 .AND. BW(I).GT. -.00001)GO TO 150
     SPXCHG(I)=100*(SW(I)-BW(I))/BW(I)
     WRITE(4,4)I,SPXCHG(I)
4    FORMAT(1H ,/,1H ,'THE PERCENT CHANGE IN FIXED INPUT SHADOW PRICE',
    1             I2,2X,'=',F8.3)
     GO TO 160
150  WRITE(4,6)
```

```
    6    FORMAT(1H ,/,1H ,'PERCENT CHANGE IN FIXED INPUT SHADOW PRICE ',
      1                    'UNDEFINED')
  160    CONTINUE
         WRITE(4,5)I,XFCHG(I)
    5    FORMAT(1H ,'THE PERCENT CHANGE IN FIXED INPUT QUANTITY',
      1                    I2,2X,'=',F9.3)
  200    CONTINUE
  201    CONTINUE
         RETURN
         END


         SUBROUTINE DWLC(NV,NF)
         COMMON/SUBIND/JSUBV,JSUBF
         COMMON/PSNQS/PV(5),PF(2),SHR(5),XF(2),BFF0(3),FQ0(2),H0(2),ZQ
         COMMON/BSVL/BY(5),BW(2),BCOST,SCOST,BFXCST
         COMMON/SUBPQS/SUBPV(5),SUBXF(2),SW(2),SY(5)
         COMMON/DWINF/SVRCST,SFXCST,SOCCST,SUBCST,DWL,DWLPB,DWLPVC,DWLPQ,
      1             BFSC
         COMMON/BEN/BNFTS
         COMMON/QUANT/Q
C********************************************************************
C
C              COMPUTE DEADWEIGHT LOSS TOTAL & PERCENTS
C
C********************************************************************
         SVRCST=0.
         DO 100 I=1,NV
         SVRCST=SVRCST+PV(I)*SY(I)
  100    CONTINUE
         SFXCST=0
         IF(NF.EQ.0)GO TO 201
         DO 200 I=1,NF
         SFXCST= SFXCST + PF(I)*SUBXF(I)
  200    CONTINUE
  201    CONTINUE
         SOCCST=SVRCST+SFXCST
         SUBCST=SOCCST-BCOST-BFXCST
         DWL=SUBCST
         BFSC=BNFTS/(BNFTS+DWL)
         DWLPB=DWL/BNFTS
         DWLPVC=DWL/BCOST
         DWLPQ=DWL/Q
         CALL DWLOUT
         IF(JSUBF.GT.0)CALL DWLFX(JSUBF,NV,NF)
         RETURN
         END
```

```
      SUBROUTINE DWLOUT
      COMMON/DWINF/SVRCST,SFXCST,SOCCST,SUBCST,DWL,DWLPB,DWLPVC,DWLPQ,
     1        BFSC
      COMMON/BEN/BNFTS
      WRITE(4,1)DWL,BNFTS,BFSC,DWLPB,DWLPVC,DWLPQ
  1   FORMAT(1H ,/,/,/,1H ,'DEADWEIGHT LOSS FROM THE SUBSIDY=',F12.2,/,
     1          1H ,33HFIRM'S BENEFITS FROM THE SUBSIDY=,F12.2,/,/,
     2          1H ,'BENEFITS AS A FRACTION OF SUBSIDY COST:',F9.3,
     3          /,1H ,'DEADWEIGHT LOSS AS FRACTION OF BENEFITS:',F8.3,
     4          /,1H ,'DEADWEIGHT LOSS AS FRACTION OF FIRM COSTS:',
     5          F6.3,/,1H ,'DEADWEIGHT LOSS AS FRACTION OF OUTPUT:    ',
     6          F6.3)
      RETURN
      END


      SUBROUTINE DWLFX(JSUBF,NV,NF)
      COMMON/DWINF/SVRCST,SFXCST,SOCCST,SUBCST,DWL,DWLPB,DWLPVC,DWLPQ,
     1        BFSC
      COMMON/PSNQS/PV(5),PF(2),SHR(5),XF(2),BFF0(3),FQ0(2),H0(2),ZQ
      COMMON/SUBPQS/SUBPV(5),SUBXF(2),SW(2),SY(5)
      COMMON/BSVL/BY(5),BW(2),BCOST,SCOST,BFXCST
      COMMON/BEN/BNFTS
      WRITE(4,1)
  1   FORMAT(1H ,/,1H ,'    DEADWEIGHT LOSS RELIES ON INITIAL SOCIAL',
     2' PRICES.',/,1H ,'    SOCIAL PRICES OF FIXED INPUTS CAN BE HARD',
     1 ' TO JUDGE.',/,1H ,'    ALTERNATIVE MEASURES OF DEADWEIGHT ',
     2       'LOSS CAN BE USEFUL.',/,1H ,'    SOME FOLLOW.')
      SHFXV=0
      SHSFXV=0
      DO 100 I=1,NF
      SHFXV=SHFXV+BW(I)*XF(I)
      SHSFXV=SHSFXV+BW(I)*SUBXF(I)
  100 CONTINUE
      ADWL=SVRCST+SHSFXV-BCOST-SHFXV
      WRITE(4,2)BFXCST,SFXCST,SHFXV,SHSFXV
  2   FORMAT(1H ,/,/,1H ,'INITIAL FIXED COSTS AT SOCIAL PRICES=   ',
     1        F12.2,/,1H ,'SUBSIDIZED FIXED COSTS AT SOCIAL PRICES=',
     2        F9.2,/,/,1H ,'FIXED COSTS AT INITIAL SHADOW PRICES=   ',
     3        F9.2,/,1H ,'SUBSIDIZED FIXED COSTS AT INITIAL SHADOW ',
     4        'PRICES =',F9.2)
      WRITE(4,3)ADWL
  3   FORMAT(1H ,/,/,1H ,'DEADWEIGHT LOSS IF INITIAL SHADOW PRICES ',
     1            'ARE TRUE SOCIAL PRICES=',F9.3)
      JF=JSUBF
      IF(JF.EQ.3)GO TO 200
      FPRT=0
      CALL APF(JF,FPRT)
      GO TO 250
  200 CONTINUE
      WRITE(4,4)
  4   FORMAT(1H ,/,1H ,'  FOLLOWING EACH ASSUME OTHER INITIAL SOCIAL ',
     1            'FIXED INPUT PRICE CORRECT')
      DO 225 I=1,2
```

```
      JF=I
      JX=ABS(I-3)
      FPRT=PF(JX)*(SUBXF(JX)-XF(JX))
      CALL APF(JF,FPRT)
225   CONTINUE
250   CONTINUE
      RETURN
      END


      SUBROUTINE APF(JF,FPRT)
      COMMON/PSNQS/PV(5),PF(2),SHR(5),XF(2),BFF0(3),FQ0(2),H0(2),ZQ
      COMMON/SUBPQS/SUBPV(5),SUBXF(2),SW(2),SY(5)
      COMMON/DWINF/SVRCST,SFXCST,SOCCST,SUBCST,DWL,DWLPB,DWLPVC,DWLPQ,
     1          BFSC
      COMMON/BSVL/BY(5),BW(2),BCOST,SCOST,BFXCST
      COMMON/BEN/BNFTS
      APFX=-(SVRCST+FPRT-BCOST)/(SUBXF(JF)-XF(J))
      WRITE(4,4)JF,APFX
4     FORMAT(1H ,/,1H ,'PRICE OF SUBSIDIZED FIXED INPUT',I2,' THAT',
     1          ' WOULD YIELD ZERO DWL=',F9.3)
      APFXCH=100.*(APFX-PF(JF))/PF(JF)
      WRITE(4,5)APFXCH
5     FORMAT(1H ,'PERCENT CHANGE IN THE INITIAL SOCIAL PRICE TO ',
     1              'YIELD ZERO DWL=',F9.3)
      IF(BW(JF).LT. .00001 .AND. BW(JF) .GT. -.00001)GO TO 10
      AWFXCH=100.*(APFX-BW(JF))/BW(JF)
      WRITE(4,6)AWFXCH
6     FORMAT(1H ,'PERCENT CHANGE IN THE INITIAL SHADOW PRICE TO ',
     1              'YIELD ZERO DWL=',F9.3)
10    CONTINUE
      RETURN
      END


      SUBROUTINE GIFCHK(NV,NF,ICALL,IG,SUBPVL,SUBPVH)
      COMMON/BEN/BNFTS
      COMMON/QUANT/Q
      COMMON/PSNQS/PV(5),PF(2),SHR(5),XF(2),BFF0(3),FQ0(2),H0(2),ZQ
      COMMON/CS/BASE,A(5),H(2),AVV(5,5),GVF(5,2),BFF(2,2),TVQ(5),THFQ(2)
     1          ,SMSHEL(2)
      COMMON/BSVL/BY(5),BW(2),BCOST,SCOST,BFXCST
      COMMON/SUBPQS/SUBPV(5),SUBXF(2),SW(2),SY(5)
      COMMON/SUBPQ2/SSUBPV(5),SSUBXF(2),SSW(2),SSY(5),SSCOST
      COMMON/ICHKR/JCHQ(5)
      COMMON/CHKR/CHQ(5)
      IG=0
```

```
C**********************************************************************
C                    SET   PRICE LEVELS TO
C                    CHECK FOR GIFFEN PROBLEM
C                    IN BASIC VALUE APPLICATION OR
C                    SUBSIDY OUTCOME APPLICATION
C**********************************************************************


C     WRITE(4,435)ICALL
C435   FORMAT(1H0,' ICALL=',I3)

      IF (ICALL.GE.0)GO TO 2900
      DO 2000 I=1,NV
      SSUBPV(I)=PV(I)
 2000 CONTINUE
      IF(NF.EQ.0)GO TO 2700
      DO 2500 I=1,NF
      SSUBXF(I)=XF(I)
 2500 CONTINUE
 2700 CONTINUE
      GO TO 3200
 2900 DO 3000 I=1,NV
      SSUBPV(I)=SUBPV(I)
 3000 CONTINUE
      IF(NF.EQ.0)GO TO 3200
      DO 3100 J=1,NF
      SSUBXF(J)=SUBXF(J)
 3100 CONTINUE
C**********************************************************************
C
C           EXAMINE SLOPE OF DEMAND FOR GIFFEN EFFECT
C                IMPOSE ZERO SLOPE IF POSITIVE
C
C**********************************************************************
 3200 CONTINUE
C     WRITE(4,436)
  436 FORMAT(1H),' GIFSET CALLED')
C     WRITE(4,437)IND,SSUBPV(1),SSUBPV(2),SSUBPV(3)


      CALL GIFSET(NV,NF,ICHQ)

C     WRITE(4,437)IND,SSUBPV(1),SSUBPV(2),SSUBPV(3)
      IF(ICHQ.EQ.0)RETURN
      IF(ICALL.EQ.0)GO TO 3600
      IF(ICALL.EQ.-1)GO TO 4000
```

```
C**********************************
C
C         CHECK NUMBER AND TYPE OF GIFFEN GOODS
C
C**********************************
      IF(ICHQ.EQ.1)GO TO 3205
      IG=1
      WRITE(6,135)
      WRITE(4,135)
  135 FORMAT(1H ,/,1H ,'SCHEME YIELDED MULTIPLE GIFFEN INPUTS')
      ICALL=0
      RETURN
 3205 CONTINUE
      IF(JCHQ(ICALL).EQ.0)GO TO 3206
      IND=ICALL
      SSUBPV(IND)=.25*SUBPV(IND)+.75*SUBPVH
      SSL=SUBPV(IND)
      SSH=SUBPVH
      GO TO 3210
 3206 CONTINUE
      DO 3207 I=1,NV
      IF(JCHQ(I).EQ.1)IND=I
 3207 CONTINUE
      WRITE(4,136)IND
      WRITE(6,136)IND
  136 FORMAT(1H ,/1H ,'VARIABLE INPUT',I2,' IS GIFFEN')
      IG=0
      ICALL=0
      RETURN
C**********************************************
C
C      HERE GOES TEXT FOR OTHER INPUT GIFFEN IF NEEDED
C
C**********************************************
 3210 CONTINUE
C     WRITE(4,436)
C     WRITE(4,437)IND,SSUBPV(1),SSUBPV(2),SSUBPV(3)
C437  FORMAT(1H),' IND=',I3,'SSPV1=',F12.6,'SSPV2=',F12.6,'SSPV3=',
C    1        F12.6)
      CALL GIFSET(NV,NF,ICHQ)
      HALT=CHQ(IND)*SSCOST/(SSUBPV(IND)**2)
      AHALT=ABS(HALT)
      IF(AHALT.LT. .003)GO TO 3250
      SSOLD=SSUBPV(IND)
      IF(HALT.LT.0) SSUBPV(IND)=(SSUBPV(IND)+SSL)*.5
      IF(HALT.GT.0) SSUBPV(IND)=(SSUBPV(IND)+SSH)*.5
      IF(HALT.LT.0)SSH=SSOLD
      IF(HALT.GT.0)SSL=SSOLD
      GO TO 3210
```

```
C************************************************************************
C               IF SLOPE POSITIVE ONLY AT PRICES
C              LOWER THAN NEEDED FOR BENEFITS
C                  RESUME BINARY SEARCH;
C               OTHERWISE IMPOSE ZERO SLOPE
C                 AND SET SUBSIDIZED PRICE
C                 AS NEEDED FOR BENEFITS OR
C                  CALCULATE BENEFITS AS
C                     SCHEME REQUIRES
C************************************************************************
 3250 CONTINUE
      TESTC=0.
      DO 3251 I=1,NV
      TESTC=TESTC+SSUBPV(I)*SSY(I)
 3251 CONTINUE
      TESTB=BCOST-TESTC
      IF (TESTB.GT.BNFTS) SUBPV(IND)=SSUBPV(IND)
      IF (TESTB.GT.BNFTS)RETURN
      IG=1
      SUBPV(IND)=SSUBPV(IND)-(BNFTS-TESTB)/SSY(IND)
      DO 3300 I=1,NV
 3300 SY(I)=SSY(I)
      IF(NF.EQ.0)GO TO 3360
      DO 3350 J=1,NF
 3350 SW(J)=SSW(J)
 3360 CONTINUE
      GIFPV=SSUBPV(IND)
      SCOST=SSCOST-(SSUBPV(IND)-SUBPV(IND))*SSY(IND)
      CALL GIFOUT(NV,NF,GIFPV)
      RETURN
C************************************************************************
C                TREAT CASE OF SCHEME GIVEN BY USER
C************************************************************************
 3600 CONTINUE
      IF(ICHQ.GT.1)RETURN
      DO 3700 I=1,NV
      IF (JCHQ(I).EQ.1)IND=I
 3700 CONTINUE
      SSUBPV(IND)=.50*SUBPV(IND)+.50*PV(IND)
      SSL=SUBPV(IND)
      SSH=PV(IND)
 3710 CALL GIFSET(NV,NF,ICHQ)
      HALT=CHQ(IND)*SSCOST/(SSUBPV(IND)**2)
      AHALT=ABS(HALT)
      IF(AHALT.LT. .003)GO TO 3750
      SSOLD=SSUBPV(IND)
      IF(HALT.LT.0) SSUBPV(IND)=(SSUBPV(IND)+SSL)*.5
      IF(HALT.GT.0) SSUBPV(IND)=(SSUBPV(IND)+SSH)*.5
      IF(HALT.LT.0)SSH=SSOLD
      IF(HALT.GT.0)SSL=SSOLD
      GO TO 3710
 3750 BNFTS=BCOST-(SSCOST-(SSUBPV(IND)-SUBPV(IND))*SSY(IND))
      WRITE(6,16)BNFTS
      WRITE(4,16)BNFTS
```

```
   16   FORMAT(1H0,/,/,/,1H ,'          BENEFITS=',F12.2,2X,'IN SCHEME')
        WRITE(4,98)
   98   FORMAT(1H ,/,/,/,/,/,
        1     '              THESE BENEFITS ARE FROM THE',/,1H ,
        2     '              FOLLOWING SUBSIDY SCHEME')
        WRITE(4,97)
   97   FORMAT(1H ,/)
        DO 30 I=1,NV
        WRITE(4,9)I,SUBPV(I)
    9   FORMAT(1H ,/,1H ,'SUBSIDIZED PRICE FOR VARIABLE INPUT',I2,1X,
        1      '=',F12.2)
   30   CONTINUE
        IF(NF.EQ.0)GO TO 41
        DO 40 I=1,NF
        WRITE(4,99)I,SUBXF(I)
   99   FORMAT(1H ,/,1H ,'SUBSIDIZED QUANTITY FOR FIXED INPUT',I2,1X,'=',
        1              F12.2)
   40   CONTINUE
   41   CONTINUE
        DO 3800 I=1,NV
 3800   SY(I)=SSY(I)
        IF(NF.EQ.0)GO TO 3860
        DO 3850 J=1,NF
 3850   SW(J)=SSW(J)
 3860   CONTINUE
        GIFPV=SSUBPV(IND)
        CALL GIFOUT(NV,NF,GIFPV)
        IG=1
        RETURN
C***********************************************************************
C                TREAT CASE OF BASIC VALUE COMPUTATION
C***********************************************************************
 4000   CONTINUE
        IG=1
        IF(ICHQ.GT.1)IG=2
        IF(ICHQ.GT.1)RETURN
        DO 4100 I=1,NV
        IF (JCHQ(I).EQ.1)IND=I
 4100   CONTINUE
        SUBPVH=1000*PV(IND)
        SSUBPV(IND)= 20*PV(IND)
        SSL=PV(IND)
        SSH=SUBPVH
 4200   CONTINUE
        CALL GIFSET(NV,NF,ICHQ)
        HALT=CHQ(IND)*SSCOST/(SSUBPV(IND)**2)
        AHALT=ABS(HALT)
        IF(AHALT.LT. .003)GO TO 4500
        SSOLD=SSUBPV(IND)
        IF(HALT.LT.0) SSUBPV(IND)=(SSUBPV(IND)+SSL)*.5
        IF(HALT.GT.0) SSUBPV(IND)=(SSUBPV(IND)+SSH)*.5
        IF(HALT.LT.0)SSH=SSOLD
        IF(HALT.GT.0)SSL=SSOLD
        GO TO 4200
```

```
4500 WRITE(4,5000)IND,SSUBPV(IND)
5000 FORMAT(1H ,/,1H ,'VARIABLE INPUT ',I1,' TURNED GIFFEN AT PRICE=',
    1      F12.3)
     BCOST=0.
     DO 5100 I=1,NV
     BY(I)=SSY(I)
     BCOST=BCOST+PV(I)*BY(I)
5100 CONTINUE
     IF(NF.EQ.0)GO TO 5300
     DO 5200 J=1,NF
     BW(J)=SSW(J)
5200 CONTINUE
5300 CONTINUE
     RETURN
     END


     SUBROUTINE GIFSET(NV,NF,ICHQ)
     COMMON/BEN/BNFTS
     COMMON/QUANT/Q
     COMMON/PSNQS/PV(5),PF(2),SHR(5),XF(2),BFF0(3),FQ0(2),H0(2),ZQ
     COMMON/CS/BASE,A(5),H(2),AVV(5,5),GVF(5,2),BFF(2,2),TVQ(5),THFQ(2)
    1             ,SMSHEL(2)
     COMMON/BSVL/BY(5),BW(2),BCOST,SCOST,BFXCST
     COMMON/SUBPQS/SUBPV(5),SUBXF(2),SW(2),SY(5)
     COMMON/SUBPQ2/SSUBPV(5),SSUBXF(2),SSW(2),SSY(5),SSCOST
     COMMON/ICHKR/JCHQ(5)
     COMMON/CHKR/CHQ(5)
C******************************************************************
C                    INITIALIZE ELEMENTS OF
C                      SUBSIDIZED COSTS
C******************************************************************
     SUMLV1=0.0
     SUMLF1=0.0
     SUM1=0.0
     SUM2=0.0
     SUM3=0.0
     SUM4=0.0
     SUM5=0.0
C******************************************************************
C                    COMPUTE ELEMENTS OF
C                      SUBSIDIZED COSTS
C******************************************************************
     DO 200 I=1,NV
     SUMLV1=SUMLV1+A(I)*LOG(SSUBPV(I))
     DO 100 J=1,NV
 100 SUM1=SUM1+.5*AVV(I,J)*LOG(SSUBPV(I))*LOG(SSUBPV(J))
     IF(NF.EQ.0)GO TO 151
     DO 150 K=1,NF
     SUM2=SUM2+GVF(I,K)*LOG(SSUBPV(I))*LOG(SSUBXF(K))
 150 CONTINUE
 151 CONTINUE
     SUM3=SUM3+TVQ(I)*LOG(SSUBPV(I))*LOG(Q)
```

```
 200   CONTINUE
       IF(NF.EQ.0)GO TO 401
       DO 400 I=1,NF
       SUMLF1=SUMLF1+H(I)*LOG(SSUBXF(I))
       DO 300 J=1,NF
 300   SUM4=SUM4+.5*BFF(I,J)*LOG(SSUBXF(I))*LOG(SSUBXF(J))
       SUM5=SUM5+THFQ(I)*LOG(SSUBXF(I))*LOG(Q)
 400   CONTINUE
 401   CONTINUE
C*********************************************************************
C                          COMPUTE LOG COST & COST
C                              UNDER SUBSIDY
C*********************************************************************
       SLGCST=SUM1+SUM2+SUM3+SUM4+SUM5+SUMLV1+SUMLF1+BASE+ZQ*LOG(Q)
       SSCOST=EXP(SLGCST)
C*********************************************************************
C                      COMPUTE SUBSIDIZED DEMANDS
C*********************************************************************
4000   DO 900 I=1,NV
       SSUM1=0.0
       SSUM2=0.0
       DO 500 J=1,NV
 500   SSUM1=SSUM1+AVV(I,J)*LOG(SSUBPV(J))
       IF(NF.EQ.0)GO TO 601
       DO 600 K=1,NF
       SSUM2=SSUM2+GVF(I,K)*LOG(SSUBXF(K))
 600   CONTINUE
 601   CONTINUE
       SSY(I)=(SSCOST/SSUBPV(I))*(A(I)+SSUM1+SSUM2+TVQ(I)*LOG(Q))
 900   CONTINUE
       IF(NF.EQ.0)GO TO 1001
C*********************************************************************
C                   COMPUTE SUBSIDIZED SHADOW PRICES
C*********************************************************************
       DO 1000 I=1,NF
       SSSUM1=0.0
       SSSUM2=0.0
       DO 800 J=1,NV
 800   SSSUM1=SSSUM1+GVF(J,I)*LOG(SSUBPV(J))
       DO 950 K=1,NF
 950   SSSUM2=SSSUM2+BFF(I,K)*LOG(SSUBXF(K))
       SSW(I)=-1.*(SSCOST/SSUBXF(I))*(H(I)+SSSUM1+SSSUM2+THFQ(I)*LOG(Q))
1000   CONTINUE
1001   CONTINUE
C*********************************************************************
C
C                        CHECK FOR UPWARD SLOPING
C                            FACTOR DEMANDS
C
C*********************************************************************
       ICHQ=0
       DO 2000 I=1,NV
       JCHQ(I)=0
       SHTRM=(SSUBPV(I)*SSY(I)/SSCOST)*((SSUBPV(I)*SSY(I)/SSCOST)-1)
```

```
      CHQ(I)=AVV(I,I)+SHTRM
      IF(CHQ(I).GT.0)ICHQ=ICHQ+1
      IF(CHQ(I).GT.0)JCHQ(I)=1
 2000 CONTINUE
      RETURN
      END



      SUBROUTINE GIFOUT(NV,NF,GIFPV)
      COMMON/BEN/BNFTS
      COMMON/QUANT/Q
      COMMON/PSNQS/PV(5),PF(2),SHR(5),XF(2),BFF0(3),FQ0(2),H0(2),ZQ
      COMMON/SUBPQ2/SSUBPV(5),SSUBXF(2),SSW(2),SSY(5),SSCOST
      COMMON/CS/BASE,A(5),H(2),AVV(5,5),GVF(5,2),BFF(2,2),TVQ(5),THFQ(2)
     1             ,SMSHEL(2)
      COMMON/BSVL/BY(5),BW(2),BCOST,SCOST,BFXCST
      COMMON/SUBPQS/SUBPV(5),SUBXF(2),SW(2),SY(5)
      WRITE(4,2000)GIFPV
 2000 FORMAT(1H ,/,1H ,'                SUBSIDIZED GOOD TURNED',/,1H ,
     1         '                GIFFEN AT PRICE=',F12.3)
C****************************************************************************
C
C                    REPORT SUBSIDIZED DEMANDS
C
C****************************************************************************
      DO 900 I=1,NV
      WRITE(4,602)I,SUBPV(I),SY(I)
  602 FORMAT(1H ,/1H ,'SUBSIDIZED PRICE FOR VARIABLE INPUT',I2,2X,'=',
     1    F12.2,/,1H ,'SUBSIDIZED QUANTITY OF THAT VARIABLE INPUT =',
     2    F12.3)
  900 CONTINUE
      IF(NF.EQ.0)GO TO 1001
C****************************************************************************
C
C                    REPORT SUBSIDIZED SHADOW PRICES
C
C****************************************************************************
      DO 1000 I=1,NF
      WRITE(4,701)I,SW(I),SUBXF(I)
  701 FORMAT(1H ,/1H ,'SUBSIDIZED SHADOW PRICE OF FIXED INPUT',I2,2X,
     1'=',F12.3,/,1H ,'SUBSIDIZED QUANTITY OF THAT FIXED INPUT =',
     2    F12.3)
 1000 CONTINUE
 1001 CONTINUE
      RETURN
      END
```

```
      SUBROUTINE TECH
      COMMON/PSNQS/PV(5),PF(2),SHR(5),XF(2),BFF0(3),FQ0(2),H0(2),ZQ
      COMMON/CS/BASE,A(5),H(2),AVV(5,5),GVF(5,2),BFF(2,2),TVQ(5),THFQ(2)
     1     ,SMSHEL(2)
      WRITE(4,1)BASE,A(1),A(2),A(3),A(4),A(5)
    1 FORMAT(1H ,/,/,1H ,'BASE=',F12.5,/,1H ,'A1=',F8.4,' A2=',F8.3,
     1          ' A3=',F8.3,' A4=',F8.3,' A5=',F8.3)
      WRITE(4,2)ZQ,H(1),H(2)
    2 FORMAT(1H ,'QCOEF=',F11.5,/,1H ,'H1=',F8.4,' H2=',F8.3)
      WRITE(4,3)AVV(1,1),AVV(2,2),AVV(3,3),AVV(4,4),AVV(5,5),
     1          AVV(1,2),AVV(1,3),AVV(1,4),AVV(1,5),
     2          AVV(2,3),AVV(2,4),AVV(2,5),
     3          AVV(3,4),AVV(3,5),
     4          AVV(4,5)
    3 FORMAT(1H ,/,1H ,'AVV11=',F8.3,' AVV22=',F8.3,' AVV33=',F8.3,/,
     1          1H ,'AVV44=',F8.3,' AVV55=',F8.3,/,1H ,
     2       'AVV12=',F8.3,' AVV13=',F8.3,' AVV14=',F8.3,' AVV15=',F8.3,
     3          /,1H ,'AVV23=',F8.3,' AVV24=',F8.3,' AVV25=',F8.3,
     4          /,1H ,'AVV34=',F8.3,' AVV35=',F8.3,
     5          /,1H ,'AVV45=',F8.3)
      WRITE(4,4)BFF(1,1),BFF(2,2),
     1          BFF(1,2)
    4 FORMAT(1H ,/,1H ,'BFF11=',F8.3,' BFF22=',F8.3,/,
     4          /,1H ,'BFF12=',F8.3)
      WRITE(4,5)GVF(1,1),GVF(1,2),
     1          GVF(2,1),GVF(2,2),
     2          GVF(3,1),GVF(3,2),
     3          GVF(4,1),GVF(4,2),
     4          GVF(5,1),GVF(5,2)
    5 FORMAT(1H ,/,1H ,'GVF11=',F8.3,' GVF12=',F8.3,/,
     1          1H ,
     2       'GVF21=',F8.3,' GVF22=',F8.3,
     3          /,1H ,'GVF31=',F8.3,' GVF32=',F8.3,
     4          /,1H ,'GVF41=',F8.3,' GVF42=',F8.3,
     5          /,1H ,'GVF51=',F8.3,' GVF52=',F8.3)

      WRITE(4,6)TVQ(1),TVQ(2),TVQ(3),TVQ(4),TVQ(5)
    6 FORMAT(1H ,'T1=',F8.4,' T2=',F8.3,
     1          ' T3=',F8.3,' T4=',F8.3,' T5=',F8.3)
      WRITE(4,7)THFQ(1),THFQ(2)
    7 FORMAT(1H ,'THFQ1=',F8.4,' THFQ2=',F8.3,
     1          ' THFQ3=',F8.3)
      RETURN
      END
```

```
      SUBROUTINE TECSET(NV,NF)
      COMMON/PSNQS/PV(5),PF(2),SHR(5),XF(2),BFF0(3),FQ0(2),H0(2),ZQ
      COMMON/ELASS/ESOREL(5,5),ELASVV(5,5),ELASVF(5,2)
      COMMON/CS/BASE,A(5),H(2),AVV(5,5),GVF(5,2),BFF(2,2),TVQ(5),THFQ(2)
     1                ,SMSHEL(2)
      WRITE(6,10)
   10 FORMAT(1H0,/,'TYPE BASE COST AGAIN. REMEMBER TO USE DECIMAL',
     1               /,1H ,' INPUTS UNLESS TOLD OTHERWISE')
      READ(5,11)BASE
   11 FORMAT(F12.3)
      WRITE(6,12)
   12 FORMAT(1H0,'IF YOU WANT TO CHANGE VARIABLE FACTOR SHARES TYPE 1;',
     1     /,1H ,'OTHERWISE TYPE 0')
      READ(5,13)INDEX
   13 FORMAT(I1)
      IF(INDEX.EQ.0)GO TO 100
      DO 50 I=1,NV
      WRITE(6,14)I
   14 FORMAT(1H0,/,'IF YOU WANT TO CHANGE THE SHARE OF VARIABLE INPUT',
     1    I2,' TYPE 1;',/,1H ,'OTHERWISE TYPE 0')
      READ(5,13)INDEX
      IF(INDEX.EQ.1)WRITE(6,2)I
      IF(INDEX.EQ.1)WRITE(4,2)I
    2 FORMAT(1H0,'TYPE THE FACTOR SHARE OF VARIABLE INPUT',I2)
      IF(INDEX.EQ.1)READ(5,11)SHR(I)
      IF(INDEX.EQ.1)WRITE(4,11)SHR(I)
   50 CONTINUE
  100 CONTINUE
      WRITE(6,15)
   15 FORMAT(1H0,'IF YOU WANT TO CHANGE ELASTICITIES OF SUBSTITUTION',
     1     /,1H ,'AMONG VARIABLE INPUTS, TYPE 1; OTHERWISE TYPE 0')
      READ(5,13)INDEX
      IF(INDEX.EQ.0)GO TO 200
      NVM1=NV-1
      DO 175 I=1,NVM1
      WRITE(6,16)I
   16 FORMAT(1H0,'IF YOU WANT TO CHANGE AN ELASTICITY',
     1 /,1H ,'OF SUBSTITUTION FOR VARIABLE INPUT',I2,' TYPE 1;',
     2     /,1H ,'OTHERWISE TYPE 0')
      READ(5,13)INDEX
      IF(INDEX.EQ.0)GO TO 175
      K=I+1
      DO 150 J=K,NV
      WRITE(6,17)I,J
      WRITE(4,17)I,J
   17 FORMAT(1H0,'TYPE THE ELASTICITY OF SUBSTITUTION FOR',
     1 /,1H , 'VARIABLE INPUTS', I2,' AND',I2)
      READ(5,11)ELASVV(I,J)
      WRITE(4,11)ELASVV(I,J)
  150 CONTINUE
  175 CONTINUE
  200 CONTINUE
      WRITE(6,7)
    7 FORMAT(1H0,'IF YOU WANT TO CHANGE ELASTICITIES AMONG FIXED',
```

```
      1      /,1H ,'AND VARIABLE INPUTS, TYPE 1; OTHERWISE TYPE 0')
           READ(5,13)INDEX
           IF(INDEX.EQ.0)GO TO 300
           DO 275 I=1,NV
           WRITE(6,18)I
      18 FORMAT(1H0,'IF YOU WANT TO CHANGE AN ELASTICITY',
         1 /,1H ,'OF A FIXED INPUT WITH VARIABLE INPUT',I2,' TYPE 1;',
         2    /,1H ,'OTHERWISE TYPE 0')
           READ(5,13)INDEX
           IF(INDEX.EQ.0)GO TO 275
           DO 250 J=1,NF
           WRITE(6,19)I,J
           WRITE(4,19)I,J
      19 FORMAT(1H0,'TYPE THE ELASTICITY OF DEMAND FOR VARIABLE INPUT',I2,
         1 /,1H , 'WITH RESPECT TO FIXED INPUT', I2)
           READ(5,11)ELASVF(I,J)
           WRITE(4,11)ELASVF(I,J)
     250 CONTINUE
     275 CONTINUE
     300 CONTINUE
           CALL SETPAR(NV,NF)
           RETURN
           END


           SUBROUTINE CHECK
           COMMON/QUANT/Q
           COMMON/PSNQS/PV(5),PF(2),SHR(5),XF(2),BFF0(3),FQ0(2),H0(2),ZQ
           COMMON/ELASS/ESOREL(5,5),ELASVV(5,5),ELASVF(5,2)
           COMMON/CS/BASE,A(5),H(2),AVV(5,2),GVF(5,2),BFF(2,2),TVQ(5),THFQ(2)
         1    ,SMSHEL(2)
      2  FORMAT(1H ,/,1H ,'I=',1I1,2X,'PV(I)=',F8.2,2X,'SHR(I)=',F5.2,2X,
         1              'TVQ(I)=',F8.2,2X,'AI=',F8.2)
      3   FORMAT(1H ,/,1H ,'I=',I1,2X,'J=',I1,2X,'ESOREL(IJ)=',F12.2,2X,
         1        'ELASVV(IJ)=',F12.2,2X,/,5H     ,'AVV(IJ)=',F12.2)
      4   FORMAT(1H ,/,1H ,'I=',I1,2X,'J=',I1,2X,'GVF(IJ)=',F12.2,2X,
         1        'ELASVF(IJ)=',F12.2)
      5   FORMAT(1H ,/,1H ,'I=',I1,2X,'BFF0(I)=',F12.2)
      6   FORMAT(1H ,/,1H ,'I=',I1,2X,'XF(I)=',F12.2,2X,
         1        'FQ0(I)=',F12.2,2X,'THFQ(I)=',F12.2)
           WRITE(4,13)ZQ
      13 FORMAT(1H ,/,1H ,'      ZQ=',F8.3)


           DO 400 I=1,5
           WRITE(4,2)I,PV(I),SHR(I),TVQ(I),A(I)
           DO 44 J=1,5
           WRITE(4,3)I,J,ESOREL(I,J),ELASVV(I,J),AVV(I,J)
      44 CONTINUE
           DO 45 J=1,2
           WRITE(4,4)I,J,GVF(I,J),ELASVF(I,J)
           IF(I.GE.3) GO TO 45
    C      WRITE(6,7)I,J,BFF(I,J)
```

```
7     FORMAT(1H ,/,'I=',I1,2X,'J=',I1,2X,'BFF(IJ)=',F12.8)
      WRITE(4,7)I,J,BFF(I,J)
45    CONTINUE
      IF(I.GE.3)GO TO 400
      WRITE(4,5)I,BFF0(I)
      WRITE(4,6)I,XF(I),FQ0(I),THFQ(I)
      WRITE(4,99)I,H(I)
99    FORMAT(1H ,/,1H ,'HI FOR FIXED INPUT',I3,2X,'=',F12.3)
400   CONTINUE
      RETURN
      END


      SUBROUTINE CHECK2
      COMMON/BSVL/BY(5),BW(2),BCOST,SCOST,BFXCST
      COMMON/BEN/BNFTS
      WRITE(4,1)BNFTS,BCOST,SCOST,BFXCST
1     FORMAT(1H ,/1H ,'BENEFITS=',F12.3,/,1H ,'BCOST=',F12.3,/,1H ,
     1                'BFXCST=',F12.3)
      DO 100 I=1,5
100   WRITE(4,2)I,BY(I)
2     FORMAT(1H ,/1H ,'INITIAL DEMAND FOR VARIABLE INPUT',I2,2X,'=',
     1              F12.3)
      DO 200 J=1,2
200   WRITE(4,3)J,BW(J)
3     FORMAT(1H ,/1H ,'INITIAL SHADOW VALUE OF FIXED INPUT',I2,2X,'=',
     1                F12.3)
      RETURN
      END
```

Bibliography

Blackorby, Charles, David Primont, and Robert Russell. 1978. *Duality, Separability, and Functional Structure.* New York: American Elsevier.

Choe, S. C., and B. N. Song. 1984. "An Evaluation of Industrial Location Policies for Urban Deconcentration in the Seoul Region." *Journal of Environmental Studies* 14: 73–116.

Christensen, L. R., and W. H. Greene. 1976. "Economies of Scale in U.S. Electric Power Generation." *Journal of Political Economy* 84, no. 4, part 1 (August): 655–76.

Chun, D. H., and K. S. Lee. 1985. "Changing Location Patterns of Population and Employment in the Seoul Region." World Bank Urban Development Department, Report UDD-65, RPO 672-91. Washington, D.C.

Diamond, Peter, and Donald McFadden. 1974. "Some Uses of the Expenditure Function in Public Finance." *Journal of Public Economics* 3 (1974): 3–21.

Eswaran, Mukesh, Kanemoto Yoshitsugu, and David Ryan. 1981. "A Dual Approach to the Location Decision of the Firm." *Journal of Regional Science* 21, no. 4 (November): 469–90.

Friedman, Joseph. 1975. *Housing Location and the Supply of Local Public Services.* Santa Monica, Calif.: Rand.

Henderson, J. V. 1977. *Economic Theory and the Cities.* New York: Academic.

———. 1980. "A Framework for International Comparisons of Systems of Cities." World Bank Urban Development Department, Report 80-3. Washington, D.C.

Kennedy, Stephen, and Jean MacMillan. 1980. *Participation under Alternative Housing Allowance Programs.* Cambridge, Mass.: Abt Associates.

Latham, Robert. 1980. "Quantity-Constrained Demand Function." *Econometrica* (March): 307–14.

Lee, Kyu Sik. 1981. "Intra–Urban Location of Manufacturing Employment in Colombia." *Journal of Urban Economics* 9: 222–41.

———. 1982. "A Model of Intra-Urban Employment Location: An Application to Bogotá, Colombia." *Journal of Urban Economics*: 263–79.

———. 1985. "Decentralization Trends of Employment Location and Spatial Policies in LDC Cities." *Urban Studies* 22, no. 2: 151–62.

Lee, K. S., S. C. Choe, and K. H. Pahk. 1987. "Determinants of Locational Choice of Manufacturing Firms in the Seoul Region: Analysis of Survey Results." *Journal of Environmental Studies* 21: 1–25.

Mayo, Stephen. 1975. "Local Public Goods and Residential Location: An Empirical Test of the Tiebout Hypothesis." In J. E. Jackson, ed., *Public Needs and Private Behavior in Metropolitan Areas.* Cambridge, Mass.: Ballinger.

Moomaw, Ronald. 1981. "Productivity and City Size: A Critique of the Evidence." *Quarterly Journal of Economics* 96, no. 4 (November): 675–88.

Murray, Michael P. 1982. "Here, There, Where: A Strategy for Evaluating Industrial Relocation Policies in Korea." World Bank Urban Development Department, Report UDD-6, RPO 672-58. Washington, D.C. Processed.

Reedy, Diane. 1985. "Empirical Studies of Intersubstitutability in Production: A Survey of the Literature." World Bank Water Supply and Urban Development Department Discussion Paper. Washington, D.C.

Virmani, Arvind. 1985. *Government Policy and the Development of Financial Markets: The Case of Korea.* World Bank Staff Working Paper 747. Washington, D.C.

Wheaton, William, and Hisanobu Shishido. 1981. "Urban Concentration, Agglomeration Economies, and the Level of Economic Development." *Economic Development and Cultural Change* 30, no. 1 (October): 17–30.